IT TAKES MORE THAN A CARROT AND A STICK

OTHER BOOKS BY WESS ROBERTS

Leadership Secrets of Attila the Hun

Straight A's Never Made Anybody Rich

Victory Secrets of Attila the Hun

Make It So (with Bill Ross)

Protect Your Achilles Heel

IT TAKES MORE THAN A CARROT AND A STICK

Practical Ways for Getting Along with People You Can't Avoid at Work

WESS ROBERTS, Ph.D.

**Andrews McMeel
Publishing**

Kansas City

01 02 03 04 05 RDC 10 9 8 7 6 5 4 3 2 1

Library of Congress Cataloging-in-Publication Data

Roberts, Wess.
    It takes more than a carrot and a stick: practical ways for getting along with people you can't avoid at work / Wess Roberts.
      p. cm.
    ISBN 0-7407-1908-4 (pbk.: alk. paper)
    1. Job satisfaction. 2. Interpersonal relations. 3. Work environment. I. Title.

HF5549.5.J63 R547 2001
650.1'3—dc21

2001022353

ATTENTION: SCHOOLS AND BUSINESSES

This book is for Jeremy, Jaime, Jared, Justin, and Christine, with my sincere hope that they will always be the kind of people others will want to encounter.

It is also for Cheryl who has helped me become more able to deal with people I would rather avoid.

It is also for the millions of people who, to earn a living, must deal daily with self-limiting, counterproductive people.

ACKNOWLEDGMENTS

Although much of an author's work is done in isolation, every book involves a team effort. To that end, I wish to acknowledge the players who had an important role in bringing this book to the marketplace.

The away team included Allan Stark, Lesa Reifschneider, Kelly Gilbert, Patrick Dobson, and John Carroll, the book's production editor, and the entire roster at Andrews McMeel Publishing.

The home team included Justin Roberts, my silent partner in writing this book. Christine Roberts, Jaime Lucas, and Jared Lucas proofread all the drafts of this book, identified errors, and made several suggestions for improvements. Jeremy Roberts line-edited the manuscript prior to its submission to Andrews McMeel. And a special note of my expression goes to Cheryl, for her assistance in developing the content for this book and for the unconditional love, patience, and support she has always given me.

CONTENTS

INTRODUCTION

It Takes More Than a Carrot and a Stick is a guide for managing relationships at work. Everyone who works has coworkers, and how we get along with them weighs heavily on the degree of satisfaction working affords.

No workplace is perfect. Some are better than others. All have people who don't get along.

At their best, relationships at work are productive for all involved. At their worst, work relationships destroy civility among all parties. Our relationships at work fluctuate between these two extremes.

How we get along with our coworkers influences the quality of our personal relationships. People who develop and maintain productive rapport in the workplace tend to enjoy better relationships outside of work: when someone with positive work relationships has an irritable day at the office, they don't come home and kick the dog in a misplaced act of aggression.

We spend more of our waking hours interacting with our coworkers than with anyone else. Our work relationships have more time to shape our attitudes and affect the general state of our emotional fitness than any other single relationship. And, given time, even the most bizarre relationships become accepted as being ordinary.

It's always easy to get along with coworkers who aren't out to destroy your self-esteem, crush your enthusiasm, or hinder you in any way. Such coworkers treat you with respect, and you return this respect in kind. The ease of dealing with such people negates any need for advice on how to get along with them. The ability to do so comes naturally.

Everyone will eventually work with people possessed by inflexible and counterproductive traits that dominate their thoughts and behavior. They can do better, but they lack the self-awareness or incentive—or both—to change. You don't have to seek these people out; they will find you. And once you know something about the way they think and act, recognizing them is as simple as spotting a Klansman marching in a civil-rights parade. Their thoughts and behavior are self-limiting, which results in their having unmet potential. They impair their coworkers' functioning, create distress in the workplace, and present extraordinary challenges to your being able to get along with them. And make no mistake: such individuals can be your superiors, peers, or subordinates. Of course, the more influential their position, the more detrimental their effect becomes, which at times turns getting along with them into a Herculean task.

In today's workplace idiom, people with self-imposed limitations are typically called "idiots." However, this pejorative panders to people with an "attitude" who are looking for a quick and easy way to rationalize their way out of taking any responsibility for getting along with anyone who thinks or acts differently than they do. But responsibility for getting along with one's coworkers cannot be so easily or quickly dismissed. No single individual is ever totally responsible for an "idiotic" relationship. All parties to a relationship contribute to its condition.

The "idiot" label is also misleading. Your inability (or unwillingness to make an effort) to get along with someone doesn't make that person a stupid or clueless fool. What is idiotic is foolishly discounting what can be obtained by trying to get along with people your instincts tell you to avoid.

Acting against instinct does not come naturally. Nor does the ephemeral, vicarious catharsis that comes from laughing at comic strips about bad bosses and malicious coworkers make us more able to get along with them or cope with the environment they create. Before we can get along with people our instincts tell us to avoid, we must first know some practical ways to deal with them effectively. And dealing with such people effectively always requires a lot of effort. It also requires patience, circumspection, tenacity, and, at times, courage.

People whose dominant traits present relationship challenges to their coworkers are as resilient as cockroaches, come in more varieties than Sybil has personalities, and survive even the deepest downturns in the business cycle. Downsizing gets rid of some, but not all of them. Reorganizations are opportunities for managers to trade these people like cheap baseball cards: they swap subordinates they don't see as having upside value for others being swapped because their own managers don't see them as having upside value. Honest performance reviews won't see all of these people out the door because there are not enough managers who have the mettle to deal with these people directly. And that's the good news.

The bad news is that, left unchecked, self-limited people multiply as fast as laboratory mice on fertility pills, especially during economic upturns. Like a few cockroaches and mice, even a few of these people can be bothersome nuisances who contaminate a healthy work environment. But a few self-limited coworkers should be the least of our worries. Roaming packs of them are much more worrisome. They have the potential to create toxic workplaces where unproductive activities, burdensome distractions, and even violence can become widespread. And if that's not bad enough, trying to get along with these people generally creates anxiety and stress that we carry home and into our personal lives.

Fortunately, there are practical ways for getting along with most anyone. This includes people who are so obnoxious that their mere presence can be emotionally draining and physically exhausting to their coworkers. And becoming able to get along with self-limited people requires you to understand how to deal with the childish, foolish, counterproductive, dangerous, destructive, and sometimes outright malicious situations they create. None of this involves becoming a self-limited person's therapist. That is better left to professionals.

This book addresses how to get along with fifteen self-limited character types that you may encounter at work. As there are no generally accepted labels for these character types, I have coined descriptive labels for them that make people who fit the description immediately recognizable.

There is no universal way for getting along with all of these character types. Firing them comes close, but terminating their employment translates into getting along *without* them rather than *with* them. And there is no guarantee that their replacements will present any less of a relationship challenge. Of course, you can always quit your job when one of these character types starts making your work life hell. However, this escapist course of action has no guarantee that you will land a job in an organization free from coworker relationship challenges, because none exist.

Sometimes people with inflexible and counterproductive traits that dominate their thoughts and behavior don't fit nicely into one type because some of their traits overlap categories. For this reason, certain ways for getting along with these characters apply to more than one type. Notwithstanding these occasional redundancies, there are practical ways for getting along with each character type. And as the types of characters described in this book cannot be totally avoided, an injection of practical knowledge about how to deal with them is just the inoculation you need for getting along with people you can't avoid at work.

CHAPTER ONE

IMPERIOUS JERKS
"The Masters of the Universe"

Domineering and overbearing, Imperious Jerks are driven by a grandiose sense of self-importance. They are so full of themselves that on Judgment Day, when they see God sitting upon His throne, they just might look up and say, "Hey, you're in my chair!"

Imperious Jerks are conceited, arrogant authoritarians who believe themselves to be unique and extraordinarily capable movers and shakers regardless of the position they occupy. They have a fascination with making big things happen, and an insatiable need for constant acclaim. They will take extreme measures to protect their fragile self-esteem, as they are easily offended by the smallest slights and become jealous and resentful of anyone who overshadows their limelight. And their overblown vanity prevents them from feeling the least bit of embarrassment when others glorify them with fawning praise.

Imperious Jerks are creatures of opportunistic necessity, which variously compels them to become pompous asses, vicious combatants, charming as a politician at a fund-raiser, or cunning as a fox stalking a rabbit for supper. Forced to choose between power or wealth, Imperious Jerks will predictably opt for power because they know power can always be used to produce personal fortunes.

Imperious Jerks are an oddity in a time when humility, corroboration, congeniality, and benevolence are highly respected personal traits. They are haughty, pushy, disagreeable, and ruthless.

On the other hand, Imperious Jerks also tend to be extraordinarily self-disciplined, methodical, intelligent, and highly competitive—traits that generally make them very effective executives. They are exceptionally skilled at networking, and they know how to leverage their relationships with influential people. They also have an uncanny ability to accomplish significant goals. And regardless of how vulgarly overpaid Imperious Jerks may be, the largest part of the bounty from their conquests goes to benefit a lot of other people—workers, investors, the community, and even customers.

As managers, Imperious Jerks tend to be impatient but capable leaders with keen "big-picture" minds driven by overweening pride. They are extraordinarily demanding of their associates and are intimidating to most people. They can be so insensitive at times that they unconsciously cause others to feel bad about themselves. And their frequent and noteworthy conquests make the occasional battles they lose in the corporate wars inconsequential.

As peers, Imperious Jerks are bullies who do what they must to outshine the competition. The unit they manage and the projects they lead are always more important to the viability of the organization than yours are. Consequently, Imperious Jerks have the boss's ear, the biggest budget, and the most staff support. This takes away from your time with the boss, dilutes your budget, reduces your staff support, and otherwise makes it difficult to compete with them, as they make certain that the playing field is always tilted in their favor.

As subordinates, Imperious Jerks are difficult to manage. They place heavy demands on your time and attention. If you don't provide them with the resources they request, they will go over your head to get them. However, if these otherwise capable associates do not easily intimidate you, Imperious Jerks will consistently perform above expectations for someone in their job.

The problem in getting along with Imperious Jerks is not just found in the extraordinarily high expectations they set for themselves and others. It is also found in their overbearing exercise of power that exploits and intimidates, stifles risk taking, confounds creativity, and gives birth to resentment rather than respect. Indeed, dealing with an Imperious Jerk can be as intimidating as facing a saber-toothed tiger when you're armed with only a sharp stick. But it doesn't have to be, nor should it.

If you work for an Imperious Jerk:

- *Understand who's in charge.* Imperious Jerk managers do not share power. You cannot win power struggles with them, so don't waste your time and energy trying. Ordinarily, no matter how off center they may be over an issue, you can't overpower an Imperious Jerk manager with facts or logic. And more often than not, wars of will with an Imperious Jerk manager end with your being fired. However, if you feel compelled to disagree with an Imperious Jerk manager about one thing or another, do your homework and do it well. There is nothing that will get you shot down faster than trying to disagree with an Imperious Jerk without being fully prepared beforehand. Going to a gunfight unarmed is safer for your self-esteem and more advised for the health of your credibility.

  If you want to be respected—treated well—by an Imperious Jerk manager, you have to bring something well conceived, meaningful, and useful to the table. Imperious Jerk managers are arrogant, but they will listen—and sometimes yield—to a different point of view, especially when they can use your ideas to their advantage. So instead of fighting a battle you can't win, become an ally and make yourself appear to be so important to your Imperious Jerk manager's success they will do everything possible to help you succeed.

- *Learn to separate tactless putdowns from constructive criticism.* Imperious Jerks are prone to indiscriminately berating subordinates when discreet feedback would be much more effective and beneficial. This predisposition can destroy your self-confidence and kill your enthusiasm if you take everything an Imperious Jerk bellows out at you to heart. Understand that this uncivilized behavior is generally nothing personal but simply their management style—their modus operandi. However, if you listen carefully, rather than tune them out completely, you will hear something amid their sound and fury that will signify a way you can improve your job performance, which in turn will always improve your ability to get along with Imperious Jerks.

- *Don't be a wimp.* Imperious Jerk managers can go through wimps faster than someone with a runny nose goes through a box of tissues. The reason for this is that wimps opt for flight rather than fight when their dignity is being stomped on. No one has the right to stomp on your dignity. Standing up to an abusive Imperious Jerk is far less risky than wimps believe. Imperious Jerks fully understand that a reputation for callously mistreating their subordinates is never offset by stellar results in any other aspect of their job.

- *Be useful.* Imperious Jerk managers develop relationships based entirely on what other people can do for them. Although they are often sloppy with details, they expect others to be thorough in every aspect of their work. This means that when working for an Imperious Jerk you need to be doing something they believe needs doing, and you have to do it well. Like it or not, it's to your advantage to make your boss look good. When what you do polishes your boss's image, it makes you look good as well. And there is no better way to get along with an Imperious Jerk manager.

If you have a peer who is an Imperious Jerk:

- *Refrain from getting into ego battles.* Imperious Jerks have very fragile egos that force them to constantly emphasize their expertise so as not to have it challenged. In a war of intellect, Imperious Jerks always lead with their résumé. Their schooling is always better than yours. They know more important people than you. And they have accomplished greater feats than you have. Of course, none of this makes them experts, only intimidators who like to bully. Competent people don't have to qualify their ideas and opinions by flaunting where they went to college, who they know, or their past accomplishments. The fact is that leading with your résumé, name-dropping, and showcasing your campaign ribbons comes across as personal insecurity rather than self-confidence. Don't be afraid to speak out on matters and issues that you understand. If you know what you are talking about, everyone will see it.

On the flip side of the coin, if the subject of the discussion is beyond the scope of your expertise, it's always better to listen and learn, because when you don't understand what you're talking about everyone will know it. And always remember that leading with your ego doesn't make what you have to say more important or credible but actually distracts from it.

- *Stand your ground.* Imperious Jerks are like bullies at school who take lunch money from vulnerable classmates. And like bullies, they will back off from peers who stand up for their right to be treated with civility.

- *Choose your friends wisely.* Imperious Jerks can't help but make a lot of enemies. Although you can't choose your peers, you can always choose which of them you want to be associated with. It is also wise to remember that despite their willingness to destroy organizational civility to achieve their own ends, Imperious Jerks are usually on the fast track and tend to get promoted ahead of their peers. This explains why you shouldn't become enemies with an Imperious Jerk needlessly. The keys here are: do your job, don't interfere with them doing their jobs, and don't try to be the group diplomat—that's your manager's responsibility.

- *Collaborate, cooperate, and communicate.* Imperious Jerks are not out to destroy you but to advance their own interests, and they don't waste their time and energy on the unimportant. Having the opportunity to team up with an Imperious Jerk on a project, even though they will always be the star, puts you under the spotlight as well. And as long as you're sharing the stage of success with an Imperious Jerk, take advantage of the opportunity to put your talents on display.

If you manage an Imperious Jerk:

- *Give them tough assignments.* Imperious Jerks have insatiable egos that feed on serial opportunities for them to be heroes. Providing them with formidable responsibility exhausts energy they would otherwise use bullying their coworkers and browbeating you. And, more importantly, Imperious Jerks generally accomplish what they set out to achieve, which means giving them tough assignments makes you look even more effective as a manager.

- *Help them play nice.* As an instinctive impulse well embedded in their basic nature, Imperious Jerks tend to badger their coworkers even after being told to stop bullying them. They just don't know more amiable ways to cooperate or to compete, and they misinterpret browbeating and intimidating their coworkers as strengths rather than seeing these vitriolic tactics as character weaknesses. Consequently, you have to keep reminding Imperious Jerks to treat their coworkers respectfully. Given such guidance, Imperious Jerks typically tone down their cavalier constitution and remit their boorish behavior—that is, until you stop keeping their egos tethered.

- *Manage rewards justly.* Imperious Jerks consider themselves as *the chosen* among their coworkers, which induces them to think they are entitled to more rewards than anyone else. They can never get enough rewards to satiate their gluttonous need for esteem or to keep their fragile egos constantly inflated. If you cave in to their incessant demands for more tokens of appreciation than they have rightfully earned, two things will happen: you will diminish your credibility, and you will dilute the standard of reward-worthy contributions you set for everyone else you manage.

On the other hand, if you don't compensate them well, Imperious Jerks will find another manager who will. Therefore, although managing rewards justly is never wrong, if you don't manage Imperious Jerks' rewards in a way that they feel is right, you will most likely lose their services. And rest assured that there are times when keeping Imperious Jerks in your service is important enough that you have to find a way to justify overcompensating them.

Getting along with Imperious Jerks is very much a matter of not allowing their haughty sense of self-importance to become an obstacle in your interactions with them. Stay focused on issues. Don't get caught up in personality clashes with them. And always bear in mind that if you can see past their obvious character flaws, Imperious Jerks make great mentors and allies who can help you achieve your own ambitions.

CHAPTER TWO

EMPTY SUITS
"The Fashion Models"

Superficial and deceptive, Empty Suits rely on their social adeptness and covert duplicity to thrive in the workplace. They are such shrewd con artists that, like infomercial spokespersons, they sometimes fool themselves into believing the illusions they create.

Empty Suits are high-strung, glib, insincere, and manipulative, and they have highly developed survival instincts. Although ambitious, they lack sufficient technical ability to succeed on their own merit. Therefore, they rely on their fine-tuned interpersonal skills and subtle guile to succeed at work the way a cheetah relies on its speed and agility to survive on the Serengeti.

Empty Suits don't take tough oppositional stands because they are uncomfortable in a competitive environment. As such, they will compromise principle to please authority figures. They are not likely to look after their associates' interests because they are too occupied looking out for themselves. Empty Suits don't cope very well when confronted about their technical incompetence, which is due not to intellectual incapacity but rather to their penchant to always opt for the path of least resistance. And acquiring knowledge—one of the most satisfying of all human endeavors—often requires intense effort.

Empty Suits are an oddity in a world where everyone is expected to add value to the organization. They would rather con than produce. In fact, their very survival depends on persuading others to do what they would rather not do for themselves—their own work. In a cynical way, this is a real art that should never be underestimated or undervalued when you are in over your head.

Interestingly, Empty Suits tend to be optimistic, making the most of bad situations. They are generally cheerful and amusing. By using their resources efficiently and working well through others, Empty Suits normally deliver acceptable results.

As managers, Empty Suits base most of their decisions on intuition instead of fact. They ask a lot of questions and look for signs of uncertainty in other people's verbal and nonverbal behavior, then decide on their course of action. They keep close tabs on their people. They are willing to delegate responsibility, but never authority. Accountability is another matter: When results are good, they are accountable. When results are bad, someone else is to blame.

As peers, Empty Suits don't earn their own keep. They hold fast to the conviction that actual work is best left to those who believe that an honest day's work is linked to job satisfaction. Empty Suits view workdays as serial opportunities to lie about their accomplishments, and they often succeed at stealing credit for the accomplishments of others and pocketing rewards that others have rightfully earned.

As subordinates, Empty Suits are much too clever to appear stupid or uninformed because they are accomplished networkers. They know what is going on and what management wants, and they possess just enough technical knowledge to talk the talk, even though they are unable to walk the walk. They are also guiltless credit thieves and recognition trivializers who would put dirt under their fingernails to further the illusion that they are making a personal contribution to the tasks at hand.

The problem in getting along with Empty Suits is not just their superficiality but also their uncanny knack for masquerading as contributors. They know they are not contributors, but they act as if nobody knows. Everyone else knows that Empty Suits are not contributors, but they pretend that they don't know. Empty Suits can be as difficult to spot as a chameleon in the woods. That is, until you can see the illusion they create for what it is: charming deception.

If you work for an Empty Suit:

- *Raise your antiseduction shield.* Empty Suit managers are able to seduce you into doing for them what you would never do voluntarily but for their smooth talking. For this reason, it is always wise to find a polite way to remove yourself from situations where you are about to be used without the possibility of any personal benefit. To lure you into their net of deception, they will chum the water with promises that they neither intend to keep nor could make good, even if they wanted to.

- *Expect to be micromanaged.* Empty Suit managers really do want their subordinates to be successful. However, they thrive on knowing what is going on all the time and therefore tend to micromanage, constantly looking over your shoulder. This tendency is aimed not at inhibiting your work but at knowing what you're doing and how you are doing it. Withholding information from Empty Suit managers is a fatal mistake that will come back to haunt you. On the other hand, the more open you are in keeping them properly informed, the more open they become in allowing you the pleasure of a little breathing room.

- *Avoid jargon.* Empty Suit managers have technical skills that are a mile wide and about a foot deep, which makes it incumbent upon you to communicate in terms they understand. Overuse of jargon doesn't impress Empty Suit managers; it just frustrates them, and they will take their frustrations out on you.

- *Be adult.* Use your expertise to help Empty Suit managers better understand the technical aspects of issues that they do not fully comprehend. Sharpshooting Empty Suits (publicly exposing their lack of knowledge) is both a constant temptation and easily done. But it will never get you ahead in the game of work and will usually land you in the penalty box. No one appreciates being put down. Conversely, everyone admires people who go out of their way to help compensate for their boss's weaknesses.

If you have a peer who is an Empty Suit:

- *Put your job first.* Empty Suits are always conning their peers into doing something for them. But no matter how much the spirit of teamwork compels you to aid your peers in accomplishing their objectives, you'll never earn high marks if the quality of your own work suffers in the process. Doing your job before assisting your peers with theirs is not selfish but is absolutely responsible self-interest.

- *Keep others informed.* The more that others (especially your boss) know about what you are working to achieve and what you have accomplished, the less likely it is that someone else can steal your ideas or take credit for your work. You don't have to brag, and you shouldn't; bragging gets interpreted as a character flaw. As with all matters, keep those who need to know about your activities informed through the normal course of how things are done in your organization. Keeping others informed is considered team play, which earns you bonus points in the game of work.

If you manage an Empty Suit:

- *Fill their empty suits.* Empty Suits want to appear competent and valuable to the organization. Nothing can make your job easier than allowing them the opportunity to acquire the skills and knowledge required to become competent and valuable to your organization.

- *Give credit where credit is due.* Effective managers achieve the greater portion of their goals through delegation and are vigilant in recognizing and rewarding subordinates who successfully achieve the assignments delegated to them. If managed effectively, Empty Suits will realize that the illusion of making a contribution earns them nothing—a fact that will encourage them to start making credit-worthy contributions.

● *Watch for red flags.* Like a little kid with a key to the candy store, Empty Suits have very few inhibitions and can become rather reckless in soliciting inappropriate favors from their coworkers, vendors, and even customers. Watch for signs of unacceptable behavior and encourage Empty Suits to keep it out of the workplace. For the most part, Empty Suits will control their imprudent impulses once they understand that unacceptable behavior will not be tolerated.

Getting along with Empty Suits is essentially a matter of helping them overcome their arrested intellectual development. If forced to earn their keep like other people, Empty Suits will become responsible for their own work and will earn credit for what they actually contribute to the organization's success. Oddly enough, work life is often too good to Empty Suits. If it weren't so, they would quickly lose their workplace niche.

CHAPTER THREE

LONE WOLVES

"The Fiercely Independent"

Impulsive and fearless, Lone Wolves are self-assured mavericks driven by an extraordinary and constant need to prove themselves. They are so confidently self-reliant that they would suture their own wounds in the emergency room at Massachusetts General.

Lone Wolves are adventurous, menacingly impatient, confrontational, and self-confident. They are nonconformists who like to do things their own way. They enjoy variety, have a need for uninhibited expression, and don't respond well in situations where they are placed under tight control or when there are restraints regulating their freedom to act.

Lone Wolves are individualists, but they are not self-centered. They truly desire to help others and the organization succeed. They are compassionate but not given to sympathy. They are persuasive and highly manipulative, and they can communicate their feelings very effectively by the use of facial expressions alone. They tend to treat competent coworkers with respect but do not suffer fools well, and they will challenge authority without the slightest hesitation, just for entertainment value. As such, Lone Wolves easily intimidate the less bold and brave, but they are never intimidated by anyone themselves.

Lone Wolves are a perplexing oddity in a time when teamwork reigns as the first rule of organizational behavior with the same immutable prominence as the Golden Rule in religion. They are not natural team players, and their independent instinct compels them to march to the beat of self-reliance without hesitation or fear of the consequences.

Perhaps because of this, Lone Wolves will take on seemingly impossible assignments—ones that would make their peers pale with fear—without equivocation. Lone Wolves also work with such proficiency that they customarily complete such difficult assignments more quickly and better than a team of their peers would.

As managers, Lone Wolves get along well with competent self-starters who require little supervision to accomplish their assignments well. They also delegate both responsibility and authority to subordinates they trust. On the flip side of the management coin, Lone Wolves drive average performers out of the organization rather than take the time and effort it requires to transform such subordinates into competent self-starters.

As peers, Lone Wolves are not suited for committee work and have very little patience in meetings. Lone Wolves consider committees a necessary evil for their coworkers who either lack the competence or the courage or both to make an independent decision. For themselves, meetings are an unnecessary evil to be avoided whenever possible. And because Lone Wolves tend to overextend themselves with their own tasks, they can't be counted on to give you a hand at your work. But you can expect them to attempt to take over your job if it adds to the visibility and challenge of their other assignments.

As subordinates, Lone Wolves get along best when supervised by someone they respect, which translates to a competent individual who will load them up with challenging assignments and give them the freedom to accomplish these responsibilities their own way. However, if Lone Wolves don't respect their boss, they will attempt to usurp their boss's authority, and they have been known to succeed at doing so. Either way, Lone Wolves are generally loyal to the organization, and when a really tough job needs doing, they will get it done or exhaust themselves trying.

The problem in getting along with Lone Wolves isn't just that they are individuals playing a team game; the combined effects of their heedless courage and their lack of team spirit first becomes self-limiting, then self-destructive. Lone Wolves can be as belligerent as George Patton was throughout his military career. But, like Patton, Lone Wolves can also be extremely beneficial colleagues once you know how to deal with them.

If you work for a Lone Wolf:

- *Take initiative.* Lone Wolf managers will forgive your honest mistakes but never your indecisiveness. If you show a little spunk and a lot of enthusiasm for your job, a Lone Wolf manager will become the best mentor you will ever have the privilege to learn from. Indeed, Lone Wolf managers are terrific at developing associates who have the will but not all of the ways to make a value-added contribution to their unit's efforts. Furthermore, Lone Wolf managers take great pride in helping associates advance their careers. And if you are willing to make an effort to help them succeed, Lone Wolf managers will provide you with more opportunities to advance your career than you ever dreamed possible.

- *Don't make excuses.* If you are having trouble meeting expectations, never go to a Lone Wolf manager with excuses or rationalizations. They view such behavior as a major weakness. A far better way to approach these bosses is to be forthright. Tell them about your problem and how you have tried to solve it. Then ask for suggestions as to how you might resolve the situation. And bear in mind that Lone Wolf managers delight in helping their associates solve their problems, but not if their associates haven't first attempted to solve them on their own.

- *Leave your hypersensitivity at home.* Lone Wolf managers are not tactless fools, but they are very candid. If candor bothers you, working for a Lone Wolf manager will be an anxiety-ridden experience. But if you respect candor and aren't into childish head games, working for a Lone Wolf is a rather refreshing and invigorating experience.

If you have a peer who is a Lone Wolf:

- *If you can't assist, stay out of their way.* Because they are individualists by nature, Lone Wolves are awful at team play. That, notwithstanding, they will commendably collaborate with others who pull their share of the load. So long as you do your part of a collaborative project, a Lone Wolf will treat you with respect and give you a hand when needed. But if you don't do your part, a Lone Wolf will walk all over you like a doormat on a rainy day.

- *Establish boundaries.* Lone Wolves don't instinctively pay much heed to organizational lines separating their turf from that of their peers. If something or someone within your territory attracts their attention as being a useful resource, they will come for it without asking for your permission. That notwithstanding, if you have the gumption to remind Lone Wolves to watch their manners, they will. And doing so will earn you a Lone Wolf's respect as someone who doesn't allow his or her village to be plundered.

If you manage a Lone Wolf:

- *Load them up with assignments.* Lone Wolves thrive on having more to do than any two, or more, of their coworkers can handle. The more challenging the assignment, the more eager they are to see it through successfully. Unchallenged, Lone Wolves become troublemakers. Routine assignments bore them. And when anxious and bored, Lone Wolves can create a lot of problems for their coworkers and their boss, which creates problems for themselves—making them their own worst enemy at times.

- *Expect candor.* If candor upsets you, don't ask for opinions you don't want to hear. Lone Wolves aren't shy when it comes to offering candid opinions, even though their opinions may be critical of those held by others. This characteristic makes them both valuable and obnoxious: valuable when critical thinking will be useful, obnoxious when the time for critical thinking has passed.

- *Keep intent in perspective.* Lone Wolves are self-limiting and self-destructive at times, but they play to win all the time. They are not mean-spirited villains who set out to limit or hinder their colleagues' effectiveness or destroy reputations. For these reasons, Lone Wolves, who are rarely aware that some of their *normal* behavior offends others, respond well to coaching directed at helping them become more aware of their self-limiting and self-destructive behavior.

Getting along with Lone Wolves involves understanding that they are fearless and independent and have a constant need to prove themselves. Interestingly enough, these traits help Lone Wolves excel at difficult, nonteam assignments. These traits are also illogical: certain situations ought to be feared, many assignments are best achieved by teams, and successful people really don't have to prove themselves all the time. Therefore, when teamwork is the order of the day, it's always a good idea to let Lone Wolves know that they don't have to prove themselves worthy to you, but that they really should constrain their stubborn self-reliance to facilitate team play.

CHAPTER FOUR

ANDROIDS
"The Blindly Obedient"

Mindless and compliant, Androids are insecure people pleasers totally dependent on other people's goodwill. They are so subservient that, like a fawn caught in oncoming headlights, they become paralyzed in situations where they must think and act for themselves.

Androids are self-conscious, submissive worriers. Androids are unimaginative, hold too humble an opinion about their potential, and have a despairing view of what will happen if they don't please others. They have an intense need to be watched over by authority figures, whom they believe are all knowing and wise and always have their best interests in mind. And in complying with an authority figure's every dictate and wish, Androids place very few restrictions on what they'll do to please. Indeed, their gullibility not only makes

Androids self-limited but it also causes them to be potentially dangerous. They often take the most offhand remark literally, and will act on it without giving the matter a second thought.

Androids internalize their personal feelings, won't speak up for themselves, and generally keep negative thoughts about other people unspoken. They don't respond well to competitive pressures, as they have a strong desire to be reassured, encouraged, and supported by their coworkers. Moreover, since Androids are too deferential to protest flawed instruction, they tend to do as they are told even if they know it to be wrong.

Androids are an oddity in a world where being assertive, spontaneous, and independent is to one's advantage. They are passive, deliberate, and dependent.

On the plus side, Androids are dutiful, follow directions, and don't try to cause problems for anyone. In addition, their desire to please can be a refreshing reprieve after encounters with coworkers out to get your job, or ones who will go out of their way to put you down.

As managers, Androids have a very hard time motivating their associates, delegating responsibility, or making decisions. As such, they tend to be stiflers of spontaneity and crushers of creativity, innovation, and risk taking—all of which is contrary to the very stuff that characterizes effective managers. That notwithstanding, they are normally decent people who want to do a good job and will try to help their associates succeed at theirs.

As peers, Androids take extreme measures to avoid interpersonal conflicts, which generally results in their not taking an active part in peer-group debates, problem-solving sessions, or decisions. Regardless, they tend to be devoted to their work and usually perform their duties acceptably.

As subordinates, Androids have a childish dependence on their manager. They need to be protected from unpleasant experiences and rewarded for every minor task they complete. They also need constant encouragement. And they expect guidance and direction in all aspects of their work. On the other hand, they are sincere in their efforts, eager to satisfy, and willing to work hard.

The problem in getting along with Androids isn't their need to please others but that their overdependency on being told what to do and how to think limits their usefulness. Indeed, working with Androids can be as irritating as having a guard dog that barks only on command. But once you know which buttons to push, Androids become easier to deal with.

If you work for an Android:

- *Take them solutions, not problems.* Android managers are too insecure to effectively cope with difficulties, but you still have a responsibility to inform your boss about problems they should know about. Rather than simply telling them about the problems you are experiencing, inform them about the steps you are taking to overcome your problems. Ordinarily, Android managers won't provide you with further insight or give you much grief about the course of action you have chosen. Under such circumstances, it's usually best to keep pressing forward. Android managers are extraordinarily indecisive, and waiting for their absolute approval will only hinder your progress. When an Android manager's indecisiveness gets in the way, it is better to ask for forgiveness later than wait for permission to do your job in the present.

• *Make reasonable requests.* Android managers are risk averse. You shouldn't expect them to go out on a limb to help you succeed. Even so, this propensity can actually work to your advantage. If you keep your risk-taking requests within reason, they will usually support your ideas, if for no other reason than to keep you happy. Then again, keeping you happy comes second to Android managers, who are always more concerned with pleasing their own boss. But if you take the initiative to find out what their boss wants from them, you can align your request accordingly. You may have to spin your ideas a little, but you should avoid becoming reckless or irresponsible in presenting them. Your plan will backfire if you provoke your Android manager into disapproving a request that a little circumspection would have helped you get approved.

If you have a peer who is an Android:

- *Include them in your activities.* Although they tend to be wallflowers in the workplace, it is always a good idea to encourage Androids to take an active role in your peer-group activities. Treating them as if they don't exist or don't matter will only lower an Android's already low level of self-confidence, which does nothing for you and hurts their feelings needlessly. Be persistent in asking for their ideas and opinions on team projects. Encourage them to speak up when it is apparent that they are holding something back. Androids are passive and submissive but certainly not stupid. And once they see that you really want their input, they will begin to be more forthright in expressing themselves and in providing you with productive support when you need it.

- *Assure them.* Androids are easily intimidated because they are unassertive and can't cope with contention. They want to be liked and will do most anything to be. But Androids go to great lengths to avoid people they perceive as posing the least bit of danger to their fragile self-esteem. Be particularly sensitive to your Android peers' need to be confident in the people they associate with. If you are kind and helpful to them, Androids will come to trust you. And when they learn that you can be trusted, Androids will go out of their way to return your thoughtfulness in both word and deed.

If you manage an Android:

- *Help them succeed.* Androids are not naturally inclined to deal with situations that require them to think and act independently. Giving them assignments that call for independent judgment, decisiveness, and risk taking before they have overcome their natural inclinations will only result in their failure to fulfill their obligations, and your failure to manage them effectively. Nevertheless, don't terminally pigeonhole Androids as associates who lack the capacity to improve. Properly managed, Androids can develop the skills and self-confidence to overcome their reluctance to think and act independently. Always do your best to make certain that your Android subordinates are qualified to perform the tasks you assign them. If they aren't, either provide them with other things to do or see to it that they receive training that will help them succeed at their assignments.

* *Teach self-reliance.* Teaching Androids to become self-reliant—independent, self-assured, and assertive—is like teaching a child to walk. It involves a lot of time, patience, and hand-holding at first. You also have to reward them for taking small steps on their own. But over time they will discover that self-reliance provides its own rewards, come to realize that pleasing others is not always necessary or best, and become less of a burden to you.

* *Communicate clearly.* Androids act on impulse, not reason. It's always best to ensure that they clearly understand any guidance or direction you provide them. If you're not sure they understand, ask them to repeat your guidance and direction back to you. This will give you the opportunity to make sure you've been understood correctly. It will also give you some assurance that they are not going to do something you really don't want to have done.

* *Ask for their opinions.* When Androids come seeking your guidance and direction on problems they are perfectly capable of solving, greet them with a "What do you think? I would like to hear your ideas." This technique will encourage Androids to start thinking for themselves. It will also be taken as a sign that you

trust their judgment. Moreover, it presents Androids with a relatively safe way to become comfortable in expressing their ideas and feelings. And the more Androids think and act on their own judgment, the more confident and self-directed they will become, which will make managing them easier for you.

- *Don't exploit vulnerability.* Androids are extraordinarily vulnerable to exploitation because they are blindly obedient people pleasers. As such, your Android staff members require special handling in order to avoid becoming victims. Place them in jobs where they can succeed and give them assignments they can fulfill. Don't allow others to take advantage of them, and do not exploit their naïveté for your own purposes. Taking undo advantage of an Android associate's vulnerability is undignified and can lead to very ugly consequences.

Getting along with Androids involves weaning them from being overly dependent on others and their heartfelt need to please. Helping them understand that they can't rely on guidance in all things is the first step in helping them overcome their deep-seated insecurity. And helping them understand that it is impossible to please everyone all the time is the first step in helping them begin to realize their unmet potential.

CHAPTER FIVE

WORKAHOLICS

"The Power-Starved"

Compelled and tenacious, Workaholics are driven by an insatiable need to feel powerful. They are so obsessed with the notion that working excessive hours builds their power base that, like coaches who run up the score after a game's outcome has been clearly decided, they will keep working even after putting in more hours on a project has become superfluous.

Workaholics are extremely tense, generally unsociable, exceedingly competitive, and overly domineering. They have a high level of aspiration, but what they ultimately aspire to is not a position of power for the sake of making the world a better place. Workaholics desire power for another reason. Indeed, power to a Workaholic is but the first link in a progressive chain of selfish motives: power begets opportunity, opportunity begets personal wealth, and personal wealth begets financial freedom—which is their ultimate goal. And make no mistake: their quest for financial freedom is guided by ruthless ambition, which impairs their judgment initially. But as they can never achieve enough power, their judgment never improves over time.

When most people talk about putting in long hours, their objective is to get a project finished. Other people have to work long hours just to make a living. And some people remain at work after hours to escape having to deal with unpleasantness in their personal lives. But to Workaholics, work is not something that can ever end. This is why being around Workaholics is like having a shark in your bathtub. They can't hide, and they wouldn't if they could. They never seem to sleep. Just as the shark must swim constantly in order to breathe, Workaholics need to keep busy all the time in order to survive psychologically. As a result, Workaholics are control freaks whose excessive concern with detail prevents them from seeing the forest for the trees.

Naturally, Workaholics tend to have strained interpersonal relationships and chronic stress and are usually too exhausted to think clearly. Their problems have a way of hindering everyone else's productivity as well. None of this bothers Workaholics, who will work themselves to death to achieve what they perceive as the pleasure of power. Yet they can't enjoy it because they are not working toward a goal; they are just working for its own sake.

Workaholics are a puzzle in a world where efficient execution of imperfect plans paves the path to success. They are so wrapped up in the mechanics of efficiency—planning, organizing, scheduling—that they actually expand the time necessary to accomplish their assignments.

In contrast, when given specific goals, Workaholics are exceptionally productive. They also work well under pressure and pay attention to the little details that often make a big difference in the quality of their and their associates' job performance. In addition, Workaholics will go the extra mile to meet critical deadlines.

As managers, Workaholics make excessive, unreasonable demands on their subordinates' time without any thought about the consequences for those people's lives. Having no lives of their own, Workaholics have a difficult time relating to such concerns. Workaholic managers don't delegate authority, because they see delegation as a way of losing control. Ultimately, the domineering, demanding behavior of Workaholic managers alienates self-motivated and competent people, creating unnecessary strife in the workplace, which ends up spilling over into their subordinates' personal lives.

As peers, Workaholics are narrowly focused on their self-interests when they should be working as a team.

They consistently overestimate their own intellectual prowess and logic as superior to that of their peers. Workaholics are greatly agitated at the injustice that some of their peers can work more efficiently and put in fewer hours, yet accomplish as much as or more than them and earn the same money.

As subordinates, Workaholics try to exert power by being overly alert to details, while sacrificing productivity by concentrating too much on how to become more efficient—without actually doing so. Workaholics suffer under deadlines because their obsession with constant work compels them to focus on trivial matters rather than the important aspects of their assignments.

The problem with Workaholics is not just that they equate being busy all the time with having power but also that their fetish for work has a way of limiting their coworkers' progress. Indeed, getting along with Workaholics is like a constant, nagging headache: it's distracting when you're trying to do your job, and miserable when you're trying to enjoy your time away from your job. But there are ways to get rid of a headache and to get along with Workaholics.

If you work for a Workaholic:

- *Set limits on your availability.* Workaholic managers believe that they have unlimited access to your time.

By answering a Workaholic manager's every beck and call, you diminish your job performance because Workaholic managers will consume too much of your productive time. In addition, you will put undue pressure on your personal life as the incessant demands of a Workaholic manager tax your emotions and energy. Let Workaholic managers know when you are, and are not, available to entertain their requests in order to avoid distractions from your duties and to minimize unwarranted impositions on your personal life.

- *Put important things in writing.* Workaholics are often mentally and physically fatigued, which makes them forgetful. Putting matters such as decisions, plans, and activities in writing is an effective way to remind Workaholic managers about what they have approved. Creating a written indication of what you are working on can also help pacify a Workaholic manager's need to be in control.

- *Don't let their personal stress be your problem.* Workaholics are stressed all the time because of their behavior and their personality. This stress makes them moody, irritable, and prone to outbursts. You should remember that this is not a business issue; it is a manifestation of a Workaholic's internal turmoil. Pay attention to what you need to do in order to get a Workaholic manager off your case, but don't expect them to ever completely let up on you. If your job is getting done, there is no reason for you to share the burden of your Workaholic manager's unending—and pointless—personal stress.

- *Meet your deadlines.* Workaholics are terrified by deadlines. When deadlines aren't met, Workaholic managers feel personally responsible, regardless of the reason why the deadline was not met. As a way of coping with this fear, Workaholics overindulge in unproductive fretting over how they feel projects should proceed. This prevents Workaholics from providing the kind of supervision that will help you make progress on your assignments. Although your Workaholic manager will vacillate between different courses of action, you should take initiative to keep the project moving on schedule.

If you have a peer who is a Workaholic:

- *Concentrate on progress, not process.* Workaholics are obsessed with meetings. To them, meetings are work because they take time, and since there can never be too much work, meetings can never be too frequent or too long. Your Workaholic peers will use meetings to analyze *ad absurdum* every intimate detail of how things should be done. Although this time could be used to actually do something, remember that a Workaholic's lot in life is not to accomplish, since accomplishment is an end. Workaholics want only to *keep working.* Do not let your Workaholic peers dominate meetings. Keep pressing them to reach the objective of the meeting; once the options have been discussed, suggest a course of action. If your Workaholic peer doesn't have a better suggestion yet refuses to agree with yours, proceed with your suggested action and let them play catch-up.

- *Involve them only where they belong.* Even though Workaholics see power as an end in itself, they usually don't meddle in affairs that do not serve their self-interest. Inviting them to review or comment on your assignments commits them to becoming too involved in your work. And once involved, it's hard for Workaholics to become uninvolved with their coworkers' activities. So if Workaholic peers don't have a legitimate interest in your work, don't ask for their help.

- *Set reasonable limits on your availability.* Workaholics are not clock-watchers. They believe that all time is work time and that your time is theirs for the taking. Instead of getting caught in their time trap, make it clear when you can be reached so that a Workaholic must conform to your schedule, not vice versa. Your being available when it is reasonable and unavailable when it is not reasonable may frustrate your Workaholic peers occasionally, but it will substantially reduce the frustration and anxiety that occur when a Workaholic hijacks your time.

If you manage a Workaholic:

- *Establish their priorities for them.* Workaholics procrastinate finishing important matters by squandering time on trivial tasks. Left to their own devices, Workaholics will never get the important things done. Managing Workaholics effectively requires you to determine for them what their priorities are. Be sure to do this in writing whenever possible; otherwise, Workaholics will slide back into their comfortable habit of frittering their time on doing work for its own sake.

- *Reward output, not input.* Workaholics believe that the longer they spend on a project, the better. When they fail to achieve a goal, Workaholics expect to receive the same rewards as if they had met the goal, since they think that doing the work is at least as important as arriving at the result that was the whole point of the effort. Although honest effort by anyone is praiseworthy, needless effort on unimportant activities is not. Workaholics, like most people, tend to favor doing that which will bring the greatest rewards to them. If you will emphasize and reward results more than hard work by itself, Workaholics will be more likely to engage more of their efforts productively.

- *Monitor their progress.* Workaholics agonize over deadlines. Their fear of missing deadlines actually contributes to their missing deadlines, since they usually find solace in wheel-spinning, meaningless busywork to avoid confronting an impending deadline. You should keep a finger on the pulse of Workaholics' progress toward meeting a deadline. This will help keep them on track, and thus reduce their suffering under the crushing pressure of having to create results by a specified time.

- *When the day is over, send them home.* Workaholics often remain at work long past the time when they have exhausted their physical and mental stamina to think and work effectively. When they have obviously put in too many hours, the responsible thing to do is to tell them to go home and rest. Making Workaholics take a break when needed prevents them from spending many hours doing shoddy work, and keeps you from dealing with the consequences of haggard thinking and wearied effort.

Getting along with Workaholics is all about preventing their need to feel powerful sour your attitude, kill your enthusiasm, or otherwise interfere with your progress. You must keep your resolve amid the artificial adversity Workaholics create, and never let their work obsession take over your own work or your personal life.

CHAPTER SIX

SLOUGHERS

"The Responsibility-Challenged"

Unhurried and indifferent, Sloughers dillydally through the day, trifling with this or that, but rarely focus on fulfilling their duties. They are so apathetic toward their work that if they were police officers, they would spend their day sitting in a patrol car with a box of donuts, relying on traffic violators to write their own citations.

Sloughers tend to be bright people who are simply uninspired by their assignments. They are more aptly described as bored than lazy. They are slothful when it comes to doing anything that doesn't interest them, but they are not irresponsible in the absolute sense. Sloughers have a knack for seeing that someone else accomplishes the tasks that are uninteresting to them.

Sloughers tend to be nice people who are unassuming, harmonious, and easy to get along with socially. Using these finely tuned social skills, Sloughers can spin their way out of accountability for not pulling their share of the load, which is less obvious than when social dolts try to weasel their way out of culpability for being lackadaisical.

Sloughers are an oddity in a world where self-starters who can multitask in a fast-paced environment are valued like an oasis in the Gobi Desert. They are easygoing, unhurried, and deliberate. It's hard not to envy a Slougher's ability to skate by, unscathed by the neurotic compulsion to do more, faster and cheaper than the competition can.

In contrast, when intellectually challenged by assignments that capture their imagination, Sloughers tend to be self-motivated, highly competent, and conscientious.

As managers, Sloughers make keen hiring decisions. They surround themselves with competent, self-motivated subordinates who require little direction or encouragement to succeed. Thus, Sloughers are able to delegate responsibility and accountability without fear of being disappointed by their subordinates' results.

As peers, Sloughers work hard to be assigned whatever part of a group project requires the least effort. Sloughers are often successful in making it seem as if they have accomplished a great deal, since they are skillful in manipulating their peers like puppets without the peers even realizing what has happened to them.

As subordinates, Sloughers tend to have more ability than initiative. This trait inadvertently leads to interpersonal conflicts with more responsible coworkers who fulfill their own assignments while having to carry the unwelcome burden of doing most of a Slougher's work. However, when stimulated by their assignments, Sloughers turn into serious contributors, eagerly engaged in achieving praiseworthy results.

The problem in getting along with Sloughers is that although they have a work ethic, they are unwilling to perform the mundane—but necessary—aspects of their jobs. This creates enmity between them and those who pick up their slack, as ultimately someone must do their routine and repetitive work—usually someone who already has done plenty of their own. Of course, Sloughers can be as unproductive as a tree sloth being used as a draft animal. But once you know how to activate them, they will do their jobs.

If you work for a Slougher:

- *Don't ask permission.* Sloughers prefer managing people who take initiative and work without much instruction or oversight. This freedom, however, does not authorize you to act foolishly or recklessly. If you have serious misgivings about an assignment, ask. But don't make a habit of seeking a Slougher manager's guidance. While they do not want you to fail, and will usually give you sound advice, Slougher managers will interpret habitual requests for guidance as a sign that you are not qualified for your job and are not the kind of self-actualized person they want working for them.

- *Report frequently, but not every day.* Slougher managers want to be apprised of the progress their associates are making, but they would rather not be bothered with daily reports of routine progression. It is enough for them to be informed of general advances toward a goal. When reports are too frequent, Slougher managers can conclude that this means they need new people, since they want to avoid the effort of actively supervising a project. Nevertheless, be sure to report any unforeseen obstacles immediately. Slougher managers depend on others for work to get done, and they are greatly annoyed when kept in the dark about a serious problem.

- *Solve problems yourself.* One of the most time-consuming and irritating uses of any manager's time is solving problems that a capable associate should be able to handle. This is particularly true with Slougher managers. Having little interest in small issues, Slougher managers are especially disinterested in addressing matters that their associates are perfectly capable of handling. You should ask for your Slougher manager to help only when a problem is truly beyond your ability to solve.

- *Lighten their load.* With their main goal at the office being to avoid working as much as possible, Slougher managers will be very pleased by associates who are willing to do work that they, as managers, should do themselves. Slougher managers are also willing to reward such efforts. By getting involved in your Slougher manager's work, you broaden your abilities and your potential for upward mobility. If you choose to offer your services to do some of your Slougher manager's work, make certain that you are actually capable of doing whatever you volunteer to do while still fulfilling your own responsibilities.

If you have a peer who is a Slougher:

- *Don't let them dump their work on you.* Sloughers can be surprisingly relentless in their quest to find other people who will do what bores them. Do not be one of these suckers. You should not feel any obligation of friendship or sense of duty to be the one who does twice the work so that a Slougher doesn't have to do any. Remember, collaboration means that *everyone* is involved in a common effort.

- *Be forthright.* If their tendency to avoid work is interfering with your ability to do your own work, let them know this. Since Sloughers assume that other people will pick up the slack without question, your admonition will often be enough to spur your Slougher peers into action. If not, at least they know that you are on to them.

- *Take the high road.* Murmuring about or dwelling on Sloughers' underperformance won't improve it, but it will diminish your character. A better way to cope with the annoyance Slougher peers present is to stay focused on your job and let your manager worry about improving their performance.

If you manage a Slougher:

- *Distinguish ability from motivation.* Sloughers tend to be more able than willing. When presented with something they want to do, able Sloughers turn into conscientious contributors. Realizing this, make their opportunity to do what excites them contingent upon the willingness to perform the mundane aspects of their job.

- *Keep them in the spotlight.* Sloughers always act more responsibly when it is expedient. Since Sloughers rely on subtly passing their work to others, they will have a difficult time pulling this off when other people can see what they are doing. Whenever possible, you should not allow Sloughers to take a position or an assignment where they can work independently and away from the scrutiny of peer pressure.

- *Tell your other staff members not to do a Slougher's work.* One of the reasons that some people are willing to do work that Sloughers should be doing is the mistaken idea that teamwork negates personal responsibility and that such perverse "teamwork" will be rewarded. Make it clear to all of your subordinates that all members are responsible for doing their own work, have no duty to do someone else's, and will not get any bonus points if they do.

- *Promote them to their level of competence.* Most often, Sloughers withhold their efforts because they feel that their best efforts are not required, since their job is beneath their potential. When you can, the best way to deal with Sloughers' lack of motivation is to give them a job that makes use of their true abilities and alleviates their boredom.

Getting along with Sloughers is easier when you do not make the fallacious assumption that someone who is bored or lazy is incompetent. Most Sloughers are potential overachievers who do not feel challenged or inspired by what they are doing—or at least *should* be doing. And the best way to get along with Sloughers is to keep them challenged by inspiring and meaningful work.

CHAPTER SEVEN

GATEKEEPERS
"The Empowerment Police"

Guarded and vigilant, Gatekeepers are officious viceroys of procedural technicalities. They are so fixated on procedure over substance that if a Gatekeeper were the last person on earth, he or she would still stop at every stop sign.

Gatekeepers are unhurried, unoriginal, and pushy. They are ritualistic rule followers who, like devout disciples of orthodox sects, obsessively abide by the letter of the law. In fact, the very idea of making decisions based on the spirit, not just the letter, of the law is so sinful to them that they will choose to follow precise technicalities to their own detriment. This is because Gatekeepers actually have very little personal power but derive what power they do have from algorithmic rules other people have established. Thus, Gatekeepers have the illusion of power but have little or no ability or desire to actually make decisions and use their own judgment—the essential elements of true power.

Gatekeepers are much like toy robots that can only walk forward when turned on. When an obstacle is placed before the toy robot, the robot, unable to turn or move back, will continue to move its legs in a vain attempt to keep going. Similarly, once Gatekeepers are set in motion, they lack the decision-making capabilities to correct their course of action—even when continuing that action is futile or harmful.

Gatekeepers are also averse to risks, and tend to be somber and unnecessarily formal in carrying out their tasks. The notion of going outside the security found in detailed policies and procedures for every possible situation gives them a case of the heebie-jeebies. This is due to the Gatekeepers' inability to function in circumstances requiring spontaneity and improvisation. In other words, Gatekeepers can't bring themselves to color outside the lines.

Gatekeepers are an oddity in a world where the ability to think clearly, a willingness to expedite decisions, and having an open mind are so vital to being able to deal with constant change. They are easily confused, obstructionist, and close-minded.

On the other hand, Gatekeepers are also careful, accurate, stable, and generally trustworthy. At times they prevent their coworkers from making foolish decisions. And, most importantly, when approached in the right way, they can actually become very helpful in expediting the approvals necessary for you to do your job efficiently.

As managers, Gatekeepers play by the book. Although placed in a position of authority, Gatekeepers aren't really leaders but followers: followers of the rules, as if rules exist for their own sake. Freethinkers tend to see rules as the parameters within which one may operate. Gatekeepers see the rules as the operation itself and enforce the rules compulsively. For this reason, Gatekeeper managers do not delegate details and they keep a very close watch over their associates' activities.

As peers, Gatekeepers, having no authority over you, seek to exert power from their favorite, and only, source: exasperating devotion to the minutiae of policy and procedure. In school, they were the kids who would say, "Teacher, you forgot to give us homework" moments before class got out on Friday. Gatekeepers don't actually help you get your work done; they create more work than you need to do.

As subordinates, Gatekeepers are shackled by the fear of making mistakes. They pay inordinate attention to detail and are meticulously neat. Gatekeepers generally do not enjoy freedom and are most comfortable in closely supervised positions. Some subordinates need to be constantly watched because they do things their own way, rather than following your instructions. Gatekeepers cause the opposite problem: because Gatekeepers are not able or willing to make decisions on their own, they will hound you for instructions on every trivial detail of how to do their work.

The problem in getting along with Gatekeepers isn't that they follow rules but that they derive satisfaction from creating needless bottlenecks and finding petty reasons to disapprove of anything that requires an independent decision. Naturally, working with Gatekeepers can be as impossible as trying to talk your way out of a speeding ticket in rural Georgia. It can be done, but not without effort and ingenuity.

If you work for a Gatekeeper:

- *Make the rules fit the situation.* Gatekeeper managers will attempt to make all situations fit the rules. Gatekeepers believe this method of problem solving to be logical, but it is not. Established rules are based on speculation about what situations will arise in the future and assumptions about what consequences will result. These things are not always possible to forecast accurately. For this reason, rules can be changed. Your circumstances (what happens to you) cannot be changed but must be dealt with as they are. In order to be effective, rules must allow for decision making when dealing with unforeseen situations. If possible, you must convince your Gatekeeper boss that the rules give you a framework within which to work, and that you must broaden the rules enough to make them applicable in a given situation.

- *Outmaneuver an unyielding Gatekeeper.* Gatekeeper managers hold back good people, which arrests potential and discourages competent workers from performing or even taking a job in the first place. When your Gatekeeper manager cannot be convinced to put the purpose of the rules before the text of the rules, you should consider going over your boss's head or avoiding your boss while finishing the job. Either way, there is some risk. Your boss won't be happy with you, but keeping your boss happy all the time is also risky. If your sole goal is to placate a Gatekeeper manager, you won't have the authority to do everything necessary to carry out your assignments, and you will never be able to do your job to the best of your ability.

- *Go out of your way to be friendly.* Gatekeeper managers, being somber and formal in both their business and personal lives, tend to have poor interpersonal skills and are uncomfortable in social situations. As a result, they usually have few friends but are starving for friendship. By going out of your way to be courteous and friendly to Gatekeeper managers, you will fill some of their need for friendship, and in return they may become more willing to bend the rules, expedite your requests, and empower you to do your job.

If you have a peer who is a Gatekeeper:

- *Don't allow them to have power over you.* Gatekeepers have a stubborn resistance to freethinking and a fear of making choices, and they will try to impose those limitations on their peers. If you allow their anxieties to inhibit your decision making, you will give them power that permits them to limit your effectiveness. Usually, the best way to deal with this problem is to ignore Gatekeeper peers' attempts to shackle your success, and do your work without seeking their consent.

- *Don't validate their moral judgments.* Gatekeepers have a concrete, black-and-white way of looking at issues. To them, there are no shades of gray, and certainly no correct choices to be found in the gray areas. Gatekeepers are seldom content to apply this thinking to their own lives only and are quick to make moral judgments about others who think and act differently than they do—even in matters not involving morality. But because the world is complex and events are always in motion, the best choice is often what you might see as a shade of gray. In addition, the "best" choice is sometimes just a matter of personal preference, and there is no absolute "right way" to complete most assignments. Gatekeepers will make moral judgments about you no matter what you do, so you might as well do your job the best way you know how and base your decisions on what you believe to be the best course of action, regardless of your Gatekeeper peers' scrutiny.

If you manage a Gatekeeper:

- *Hold them personally accountable.* Gatekeepers will use policies and procedures to excuse themselves from personal responsibility. Whenever their actions lead to undesirable consequences, Gatekeepers will be quick to point out that they were doing as they were told. However, you should remember that Gatekeepers are not perfectly following the rules, just their own interpretations of the rules. Different people can interpret the same rules in different ways, and still believe that their own understanding is the correct one. Additionally, despite their efforts to get out of it, Gatekeepers cannot avoid making decisions. Doing what you are told, or what you believe you were told, is in fact a decision. Every decision brings consequences, and there is no valid reason why Gatekeepers should be able to escape the responsibility for what they do.

- *Force them to take initiative.* The purpose of delegating tasks is to enlist other people to help you get your job done. In order to delegate, you must be able to assume that your subordinates will take initiative to do their work. Gatekeepers challenge this assumption, because their reluctance to make decisions on their own results in their constantly asking for your guidance in every detail of their assignments. If you allow Gatekeeper staff members to pester you repeatedly with excessive attention to detail and their need for constant attention, neither you nor they will have enough time to do your jobs well. Gatekeepers are more able than willing, and sometimes the most practical way to get along with them is to tell them to figure it out for themselves.

- *Keep them from becoming obstacles to others.* Your staff members have a right to do their work without unnecessary interference from you. Indeed, if you allow Gatekeepers to be in a position where they constantly inhibit the effectiveness of their associates, you are enabling the Gatekeepers to be an unnecessary interference. Although you can't control every way in which Gatekeepers interfere with others' work, you should never put Gatekeepers in a position where they have the actual authority to prevent their coworkers from taking the action necessary to fulfill their duties.

Getting along with Gatekeepers requires you to understand that rules, policies, and procedures exist to give you a framework in which to act, not to imprison your ability to act. Once you understand this, you are much less likely to be persuaded by the Gatekeepers' fallacy that rules are an end to themselves. You should also consider that despite all your efforts, sometimes Gatekeepers really can prevent you from going forward. Don't allow this to become a battle of willpower. By focusing on your goal, you are more likely to find a way around those Gatekeepers who refuse to yield.

CHAPTER EIGHT

FAULTFINDERS

"The Self-Righteous"

Sanctimonious and inflexible, Faultfinders are secretive, self-appointed members of the morality police. They are so zealously concerned with the slightest defect in other people that they would support putting television cameras in everyone else's house to make sure that nobody is doing something bad.

Faultfinders are extremely reserved, inflexible, and sycophantic. They tend to be deliberate, easily offended, and hypocritical. Faultfinders are severely judgmental but take evasive action to avoid being judged themselves—like a parishioner who confesses a fellow parishioner's sins to divert notice from his own.

Faultfinders have a holier-than-thou preoccupation with thoughts and behaviors that are unacceptable to them. They distort the significance of anything they find disagreeable and usually overreact to the honest mistakes of their coworkers. As if this weren't bad enough, their self-initiated spying and clandestine reports to management create an atmosphere of suspicion and distrust. Ironically, to Faultfinders' way of thinking, betraying their coworkers' trust is morally responsible. This is why when Faultfinders get caught red-handed in their spy-and-tattle activities, their skin doesn't crawl with guilt or shame. They simply deny any wrongdoing without any pangs of conscience.

Faultfinders are an oddity in a world where minding your own business is an effective way to get along with your coworkers. They think that it is their duty to divulge to their boss the slightest flaw in their coworkers' behavior.

On a more positive note, Faultfinders tend to be deferential to authority and dedicated to their jobs and can be quite productive when placed in closely supervised positions that require little interaction with their coworkers.

As managers, Faultfinders are rigid, authoritative, and hyperalert to anything out of the ordinary. They are averse to taking risks and terrified of making the slightest mistake, since they interpret mistakes as an indication of corrupt moral character instead of a fact of life from which no one is spared. They are also cold and humorless, and they restrict their compassion to persons who think and act as they do.

As peers, Faultfinders deflect attention away from their own inadequacies by ratting out their coworkers. Being sneaky snitches makes them difficult to spot, which breeds an atmosphere of suspicion that creates general distrust and CYA (cover your ass) behavior. Any one of these conditions, isolated from all the others, distracts from your ability to have an otherwise productive rapport with Faultfinders. Linked together, this chain of distracting behavior becomes a disruptive force in your relationships with them.

As subordinates, Faultfinders are edgy, threatened by change, and envious of attention received by their coworkers. They cast themselves in the role of the manager's remote eyes and ears. Although they believe this to be righteous intervention, the effects of their confidential tattling on "sinful" coworkers are at the least disruptive and at the most destructive.

The problem in getting along with Faultfinders is not just that they are filled with self-doubt and require constant reassurance from their boss but also that, left unchecked, they can transform a decent work environment into one polluted with petty bickering, widespread suspicion, cynical distrust, and needless stress. However, Faultfinders are like ants at a picnic, in that they are more of a pest than a plague once you know how to deal with them.

If you work for a Faultfinder:

- *Refuse to spy.* Faultfinder managers attempt to get their associates to spy on their coworkers and report back every little "sin" that is secretly observed. Although spying may endear you to a Faultfinding manager, it will certainly estrange you from everyone else. The first time you rat out a coworker to a Faultfinder manager you become a confidential source that will be continually pumped for similar information in the future. Better than spying on your coworkers, always be too busy doing your job to notice what others may be doing wrong.

- *Be discrete.* Whatever you say to a Faultfinder manager can be used against you and, quite possibly, against your coworkers. Communication with a Faultfinder manager is best kept strictly to business, and specifically to that business that needs discussing. Although you can't refuse to communicate with your boss and still keep your job, the more you volunteer unnecessary or inappropriate information, the easier it becomes for Faultfinder managers to use what you say in a way that will wreck otherwise healthy relationships between you and your coworkers.

- *Don't sweat the boss stuff.* Faultfinder managers make terrible bosses because they are incapable of simultaneously fulfilling their self-appointed role as morality police and effectively managing their unit. Nor can they retain good people for very long. However, if you can cope with a Faultfinder boss in the short term, you don't have to sweat having one as your boss in the long term. Faultfinder managers are not an endangered species, but they rarely remain in management positions for any great length of time.

If you have a peer who is a Faultfinder:

- *Show some grit.* If a Faultfinder is causing you problems, direct confrontation will sometimes remedy the situation because, like rats, Faultfinders operate best in the dark. Letting Faultfinders know that you are aware of what they are up to and that you are not going to put up with it strikes at the heart of their false sense of power. If you feel that direct confrontation will only make matters worse, you can always go to your boss. However, besides the fact that you can't always count on your boss to intervene in your favor, going to your boss over trivial matters tends to aggravate a healthy working relationship. You just have to deal with these situations the best you can under the circumstances. This is not terribly consequential, though it is always frustrating.

- *Avoid retaliation.* If you are suffering at the hands of a Faultfinder, remember: getting sucked into the fault-finding game only makes matters worse. As the saying goes, "Never mud wrestle with a pig. You both get dirty, and the pig likes it."

If you manage a Faultfinder:

- *Expect them to tell on you.* Being ratted out every now and then is simply part of management life. Most managers aren't likely to think any less of you for it and will find a way to help the Faultfinder understand that such nefarious behavior is both inappropriate and unacceptable. However, having discovered that a Faultfinder subordinate is operating behind your back, don't allow it to continue with impunity. At the same time, make sure to build a trusting relationship with your boss before a Faultfinder brings your reputation into question.

- *Don't encourage tattletales.* Listening to Faultfinders' tattles only reinforces this behavior, which increases the likelihood that they will be back with more tales to tell. A helpful technique for a manager in this situation is to say something like "I don't want to hear about Jaime's [or whoever's] problems right now. Let's talk about you. How are you doing? What are you working on improving?"

- *Put an end to the problem quickly.* Should you manage a Faultfinder who is causing problems, take immediate action. The longer you delay taking corrective measures, the worse the problems will become. People who have time to spy on their coworkers are either not paying enough attention to their own work or don't have enough work to keep them busy.

- *Be circumspect.* Don't overreact to what Faultfinders snitch to you. Police detectives might get excited over what one of their snitches tells them, but having informers in the workplace is a real problem that is worsened by overreacting to what they report. However, if a Faultfinder tells you about something that might require your attention, look into the matter independently. Never assume that Faultfinders are telling you the whole truth about anything they have to say about a coworker's behavior.

Getting along with Faultfinders requires helping them focus on matters of their legitimate concern. Encourage them to spend time working instead of spying, as the more time they spend working, the more effective they will become at their jobs. And when people are performing their own jobs effectively, they don't have time to find fault with their coworkers.

CHAPTER NINE

BUNGEE JUMPERS
"The Thrill Seekers"

Theatrical and easily distracted, Bungee Jumpers are driven by an uncontrollable, incessant need to try something new and sensational. They are so impulsive in this regard that they will mindlessly follow momentary fads, like the mesmerized children of Hamelin marching behind the Pied Piper.

Bungee Jumpers tend to be haphazard in both thought and action, and they are attracted to activities that are exciting and stimulating but serve no real purpose. They are forgetful and have short attention spans, which makes it difficult for them to concentrate. They are also overexcitable, talkative, and predictably unpredictable.

Bungee Jumpers have a deep-seated need to be the center of attention, which causes them to interrupt other people's conversations and to alternatively tease and coerce just to gain notice. They have dramatic and colorful ways of expressing themselves, are adept at making their ideas and opinions seem more important than they really are, and sprinkle normal discourse with psychobabble. They become frustrated when their thoughts are scrutinized, which exposes their socially insensitive predisposition. And when Bungee Jumpers are faced with a stressful situation, their typically upbeat mood deteriorates as the pressure they feel intensifies.

Bungee Jumpers are an oddity in a world where being self-managed, goal-directed, thorough, and punctual is given so much emphasis. They require close supervision, have difficulty with goal-directed activities, are inattentive to significant details, and do not complete their assignments on time.

Bungee Jumpers will, however, perform adequately in structured environments with minimal distractions. They are divergent thinkers, a trait that expedites their creative nature. They are also naturally well-intentioned people who do not willfully offend others.

As managers, Bungee Jumpers tend to be unorganized and poor planners. They will overcommit their resources by taking on more projects than they can manage or their subordinates can handle. They monitor their subordinates' performances only sporadically, since they expend too much of their time and attention on activities that are playful and stimulating but distracting. Bungee Jumper managers become serious and impatient when they want something done, though they often forget what they asked for before it can be accomplished.

As peers, Bungee Jumpers are romantics who rely on others to rescue them when they are in over their heads. They disrupt their peers' activities and often speak out of turn. They do not like to talk about their problems and can become aggressive for inconsequential reasons. Still, Bungee Jumpers are easily embarrassed and become apologetic when confronted with their improper behavior. They will also betray their coworkers for personal gain, which makes it hard for them to maintain consistently productive relationships.

As subordinates, Bungee Jumpers are high-spirited and amusing, yet they do not have sufficient self-discipline to work independently. They are easily confused and typically need instructions to be repeated. They have superficial knowledge about many things but expertise in very little. However, they are generally more capable than their performance indicates. Bungee Jumpers are just too flighty and careless to use their abilities skillfully. Bungee Jumpers are not the kind of subordinates who solve their own problems, but they do have vivid imaginations and often suggest ideas worthy of further consideration. And they are gregarious individuals who work best in team environments.

The problem in getting along with Bungee Jumpers isn't their flirtation with different ideas or their involvement in exciting activities but their craze for constant stimulation that distracts them from paying proper attention to their basic job responsibilities. In fact, working with Bungee Jumpers can be as exasperating as trying to teach arithmetic to a child on a sugar high. But once they understand that fulfilling their basic job responsibilities has more lasting value than tasting the latest trend, Bungee Jumpers become more productive.

If you work for a Bungee Jumper:

- *Fill in the gaps in their managerial observations.* Bungee Jumper managers are short on management insight because they don't think beyond the obvious. Take the initiative to suggest "out-of-their-comfort-zone" solutions for problems to which the answers are beyond their managers' understanding. Not only will this compensate for your managers' arrested problem-solving skills, it will free you from the bondage of having to endure the effects of their incompetence. Usually, Bungee Jumper managers don't balk at, fret over, or punish any suggestions that help them deal with issues and problems beyond their ability to manage effectively.

- *Lend a basic management hand.* Bungee Jumper managers are too flighty to perform fundamental management tasks that require some degree of concentration and forethought. Rather than be victimized by this sad state of affairs, volunteer to help your Bungee Jumper manager organize and plan projects and activities. Don't worry; they will appreciate your assistance. Besides being a good way to help Bungee Jumper managers do their job, it puts you in a position to advise them when their unit's plate is full and there is no room for further commitments. It will also provide you with preparatory practical experience for broader responsibilities.

- *Be diplomatic.* Bungee Jumper managers' need for constant stimulation causes them to call unnecessary meetings, engage others in impertinent small talk, and make spur-of-the-moment requests that are of no consequence. None of this has a mean-spirited intention. However, such activities can be disruptive. When they are, find a diplomatic way to excuse yourself from participating in them. You won't be able to talk your way out of all such disruptions, but avoiding just a few of them will be a boost to your productivity.

- *Attend their social gatherings.* Bungee Jumper managers take pleasure in sponsoring social activities. It gives them an opportunity to be the center of attention and to share their enthusiasm for diversion. Although attendance at these functions is rarely required, taking part in them allows you an opportunity to benignly nurture your manager's need for attention and to get to know your coworkers better. Both of these opportunities usually benefit you with improved relationships at work. And don't overlook the fact that many of these functions can be enjoyable as well. However, if you can't or don't want to attend one of these activities, inform your manager in advance. Just not showing up can be interpreted in negative ways that will harm your relationships with your manager and coworkers.

If you have a peer who is a Bungee Jumper:

- *Teach them how to solve problems.* Bungee Jumpers routinely encounter problems they are not prepared to address and will try to seduce someone into dealing with the situation for them. As your peers' success is often linked to your own, you really shouldn't want one of them to fail. Although it is sometimes easier to just solve their problem than to tutor them through it, taking responsibility for their problem fails to help them become more able to solve problems in the future. Offering advice or showing them how to do something is always good, but make sure you stop short of doing their work.

- *Don't put up with a nuisance.* Bungee Jumpers can find many ways to disrupt your work-related activities. If Bungee Jumper peers are needlessly bothering you, tell them to go away. You don't have to be rude about it. Just tell them you don't have time for disruptions at the moment. Bungee Jumpers embarrass easily and will usually take the hint and let you be. If they do take some offense, don't worry about it. Bungee Jumpers can be annoying at times, but they are generally decent people, and it's unusual for decent people to hold a grudge or be vindictive.

- *Enjoy the show.* Despite being short on substance, Bungee Jumpers have a way of making dramatic presentations that overstate the obvious with flair. Rather than letting these instances become an aggravating interlude in a busy day, take a few minutes to enjoy the entertaining value that comes from watching Bungee Jumpers put their lack of depth on display. Sure, teamwork is a serious matter, but you needn't be serious over all matters that arise out of team play. Of course, if the subject is important, offer a helpful critique after you've enjoyed the show.

If you manage a Bungee Jumper:

- *Train and retrain.* Different people learn the same skills at different rates, and having the patience to accommodate individual differences is an excellent management trait. Bungee Jumpers are far from unteachable, but their natural inability to concentrate lengthens the time required for them to learn how to perform some of their basic job duties. Bringing out the best in Bungee Jumpers necessitates training and retraining until they develop the ability to execute the tasks they are to perform. The most efficient way to train Bungee Jumpers is to make their training intense, crammed with practical exercises overseen by corrective feedback and conducted in a place as distraction-free as possible. And don't be hesitant to send an underachieving Bungee Jumper back for retraining.

- *Structure their environment.* Bungee Jumpers perform best in highly structured work environments with minimal opportunities to wander in mind or body. They also do best when they understand what is expected of them, when their assignments are due, and that they are not free to roam as they please. This may require more of your time than you feel you should spend managing one subordinate. However, successful managers do what it takes to manage every subordinate effectively. You can save some of your own time in this regard by placing Bungee Jumpers on teams where their teammates will help keep them on task.

- *Demand attention to detail.* Bungee Jumpers are too reckless to pay attention to details on their own, which can lead to unsatisfactory results. Managing Bungee Jumpers requires you to keep their attention focused on the critical details of their duties. As they are forgetful at times, it's a good idea to provide Bungee Jumpers with written instructions or to have them take notes. Teaching Bungee Jumpers to pay attention to detail is a quick way to help them develop both the attention span and the discipline to become more self-managed.

- *Keep an open mind.* Bungee Jumpers are inquisitive and imaginative, which causes them to color outside the lines when most everyone else is thinking in conventional terms. They also have dramatic ways of making their ideas known. But if you are not fooled by theatrics or confused by psychobabble, Bungee Jumpers often have inventive thoughts on everyday subjects and innovative alternatives to the way things are ordinarily done. If you want to capitalize on a Bungee Jumper's resourcefulness to you, you have to be willing to keep an open mind.

Getting along with Bungee Jumpers involves helping them become more aware of the constant thrill that comes from knowing how to do their work and from successful execution of their duties. It also requires that you avoid being manipulated by their theatrics. And the sooner Bungee Jumpers understand that self-discipline is more stimulating than being disciplined, the more motivated they will be to meet performance expectations.

CHAPTER TEN

PERPETUAL VICTIMS
"The Whiners and Bitchers"

Peevish and bitter, Perpetual Victims are bellyachers whose prominent trait is an inability to cope with the least bit of adversity. They are such chronic complainers that they would moan over having to pay taxes on the proceeds from a million-dollar winning lottery ticket that they bought for a buck.

Perpetual Victims are extremely high-strung, impatient, and emotionally erratic. They are self-effacing to the point that they don't pursue their own rights but protest when others take advantage of them. They are easily frustrated, blame others for their problems, are generally unsociable, and become more excited than a buzzard on a fresh road kill every time they can find an excuse to harp about one thing or another. They are also pessimists who take life too easily, as they always expect the worst and do nothing to prevent it from happening. Perpetual Victims obsess over what they don't have instead of recognizing chances to build on what they do, which blinds them to the sky of opportunity that looms above the clouds of adversity in everyone's life.

Perpetual Victims tend to be suspicious of others, which prevents them from developing trusting relationships. They experience excessive emotional anxiety over any event that causes them to feel as if they have been mistreated. Conversely, they are inconsiderate of their coworkers' feelings, but they want others to like them. Even so, their incessant moaning and groaning along with their snide comments prevent others from wanting to associate with them.

Perpetual Victims are a paradox in a time when the ever-present opportunity to improve one's lot in life has never been greater, because instead of trying to do something about a bad situation, they will adapt to it. No matter what they have to build on or the opportunities that come their way, Perpetual Victims always feel shortchanged. And, oddly enough, they actually enjoy being seen as victims because they thrive on the attention it affords them.

On the flip side, Perpetual Victims are often self-disciplined, thorough, and organized, hard workers when it comes to performing their assignments. And, curiously,

they are quite capable of giving solid advice to coworkers who are experiencing job-related problems.

As managers, Perpetual Victims are the kind of
bosses who make you dread going to work. They arrive
on the job each morning preoccupied by the persistent
belief that something bad is going to happen. And
quicker than a lightning strike, they will unleash their
hostilities indiscriminately. The good news is that, with
rare exception, their relentless carping and fatalistic attitude exclude Perpetual Victims from being placed in
management positions.

As peers, Perpetual Victims are unpleasant workplace companions that are difficult to tolerate. They are
quick to attribute blame for personal shortcomings to
their coworkers, whom they tend to see more as foes
than allies. They are also suspicious of good intentions
because they believe their coworkers are out to get them.

As subordinates, Perpetual Victims are difficult to
manage. They have a distorted perception about the
value that their boss places on listening to complaints.
They are also inflexible and overly demanding of their
coworkers' attention. They tend to insist on doing
things their way, and will threaten to quit when they
either can't have their way or aren't getting enough sympathy from their manager and coworkers.

The problem in getting along with Perpetual Victims
is not just that they whine and bitch about every little

thing at work but also that their incessant misery prevents them from dealing with work life's lumps and acting on the opportunities that come their way. In truth, working with Perpetual Victims can be as excruciating as trying to answer questions while a dentist is drilling out a cavity without having first injected you with a painkiller. A despicable thought, but you can't always distance yourself from people who cause you stress.

If you work for a Perpetual Victim:

- *Carry an emotional umbrella.* Perpetual Victim managers can't refrain from griping and grumbling. They don't know any other way to address even minor inconveniences. You know it's coming; it's only a matter of when. So when a Perpetual Victim manager starts in on you for no legitimate reason, let it roll off your back. If you take their biting criticism to heart, you will start feeling like a helpless victim yourself. In fact, every now and then it's a good idea to smile and thank Perpetual Victim managers for their belittling observations. Doing so will confuse them because they expect you to act downtrodden. But when they can see that their carping at you bothers you not at all, Perpetual Victim managers will usually find someone else to pick on, because they actually get a charge out of making others feel poorly about themselves.

- *Reject undue criticism.* Perpetual Victims have a way of going overboard and attacking others' dignity. You don't have to tolerate such attacks from your manager, and you really shouldn't. Besides, standing up to Perpetual Victim managers is not as fearsome as it may seem on the surface. They will dish out nasty remarks only to people unwilling to stand up for their right to be treated with respect. Tell Perpetual Victim managers that you will listen to what they have to say but that you won't tolerate personal insults. You might be surprised at how quickly this will change your relationship.

- *Be cheerful and productive.* Perpetual Victim managers have more ways to express their misery than the IRS has to tax your income. But when you cheerfully perform your duties well, there is no reason to worry about your manager's personal problems or a job-performance audit. Moreover, when you're cheerful and productive Perpetual Victim managers will stay out of your way, since they love to spread misery and can't deal with happy people. Although it is generally a good idea to discuss work-related problems with your manager, you are usually better off seeking advice from someone other than a Perpetual Victim manager. This is not to say that you should lie about your problems. But you don't have to disclose the problems that you can get someone else to help you solve before they have to become a topic of discussion between you and your Perpetual Victim manager.

If you have a peer who is a Perpetual Victim:

- *Avoid complaint sessions.* Perpetual Victims love to complain, and will complain to anyone willing to listen. You can't avoid interacting with your peers, but there are times when you are better off telling them that their personal problems are none of your business. Listening to someone else gripe about their problems solves nothing. Nor does listening to someone's grumbling make you more effective at your job. But it will distract from your own productivity. And if you listen to too much complaining, sooner or later it will sour your attitude about your coworkers, your job, your organization, and life in general.

- *Don't be a scapegoat.* In an attempt to escape accountability, Perpetual Victims attribute their mistakes and shortcomings to peers at every opportunity. You have to tell Perpetual Victim peers that you are not going to accept responsibility for problems of their own doing. Telling them no doesn't have to turn into a shouting match, but you have to be firm. Furthermore, when they can't find a scapegoat, Perpetual Victims begin to understand that they play an important role in creating many of the problems they face.

- *You don't have to like them.* As much as it goes against the grain of opinion in some circles, peers don't have to be friends in order to have a productive relationship at work. It is also true that becoming too close to your peers can result in a loss of objectivity in situations that call for cold logic over emotional attachment. Either way, there is no secret about the fact that Perpetual Victims have personality kinks that make it rather difficult for them to form workplace friendships in the first place. Nevertheless, you can maintain productive relationships with them. Treat them as if they are important to your success, because they are. Take time to assist them with their assignments when appropriate. Ask for their opinion when you could use another point of view. Include them in work-related social activities. And always thank them on occasions when they lend you a helping hand.

If you manage a Perpetual Victim:

- *Team them up with positive peers.* Misery does love company, but in the company of positive peers, Perpetual Victims tend to adapt to good circumstances just as naturally as they adapt to bad situations. Keep in mind that, like most everyone else, Perpetual Victims really do want to be liked. They just don't have a lot of savvy when it comes to behaving in ways that make others want to like them. So since peer pressure is such a powerful force, use it to your advantage by teaming Perpetual Victims up with positive peers at every opportunity. This will not only bring out the best attitudinal behavior in Perpetual Victims but will actually begin to reshape how they feel about themselves and think about life.

* *Don't confuse attitude with aptitude.* Perpetual Victims always lead with their worst side—their bad attitude. Although this is a real turnoff and can make you think they are inept, Perpetual Victims tend to be very competent performers and are usually willing to learn new skills. To get the most out of Perpetual Victims, you have to make the most of their abilities. Assign them meaningful tasks. Keep them busy. Reward them properly. But if Perpetual Victims' attitudes are getting in the way of their effectiveness or causing problems with their peers, confront the situation directly. Don't cut Perpetual Victims a lot of slack when their need for suffering is contaminating their coworkers' attitudes. On the other hand, make it a point to catch Perpetual Victims when they aren't complaining and tell them that you and others appreciate their cheerful attitude.

- *Redirect their complaints.* Perpetual Victims are always complaining about this or that, but rarely about anything worthy of attention. Instead of allowing them to dwell too long on the negative, which always makes matters seem worse than they really are, redirect Perpetual Victims' complaints by asking them about what is going well for them. They may have some difficulty coming up with positive experiences to share with you at first, as Perpetual Victims don't look for the good in life. However, the more you ask for good news, the more good news Perpetual Victims will find to share with you. And when they start looking for positive experiences to share with you, Perpetual Victims will begin to see the good in situations.

- *Teach them how to deal with adversity.* One of the primary reasons why Perpetual Victims don't know how to be happy is that they don't know how to deal with adversity effectively. The fallacy in Perpetual Victims' thinking is that fate has singled them out and showered them with overwhelming challenges. In reality, all of us face adversity—but not all of us choose to be victimized by the facts of life. In order to manage Perpetual Victims effectively, help them understand that you expect all of your associates to overcome difficulties in the workplace. Although training is crucial for showing Perpetual Victims how to solve problems, remember that their attitude, not their ability, is the main factor that keeps Perpetual Victims from overcoming obstacles. Show Perpetual Victims that their sincere, meaningful efforts are appreciated—and required. You should also be certain that your expectations are reasonable and prudent, so that Perpetual Victims have no basis for claiming that your expectations simply can't be met. Perpetual Victims can be much more productive and tolerable when they recognize the incentives for dealing with the situation instead of just whining about it.

Getting along with Perpetual Victims involves helping them shape a positive outlook toward their work and coworkers. Although they struggle with seeing the good, once you help them begin to experience the rewards of taking responsibility for their behavior, Perpetual Victims acquire the ability to view life in more optimistic ways. This will make getting along with them much more bearable.

CHAPTER ELEVEN

COLLEAGUE SLAYERS

*"The Backbiters, the Rumormongers,
and the Saboteurs"*

Predatory and venomous, Colleague Slayers are relentless snoops who poke and probe for ways to destroy their coworkers' reputations with the dogged tenacity of tabloid reporters sifting through celebrities' trash containers. They are so evil that Heaven doesn't want them and the Devil is afraid they'll take over Hell.

Colleague Slayers are self-centered, ruthless, methodical villains. As such, they are not bothered in the least by lying, stealing, or cheating. Even so, Colleague Slayers are generally discriminating when it comes to showing their fangs. They normally attack only those colleagues who have offended them or present a competitive threat to them in the battle for power and prestige that occurs in virtually all workplaces. They also have paper-thin egos, are easily threatened, and have a profound need for the kind of recognition and praise they would never shower on a coworker. Although they are not ones to walk away from a fight, Colleague Slayers turn into cowards the very moment they realize they cannot win.

Disarmingly polite and pleasant toward their allies, Colleague Slayers are as unrestrained as crack addicts on a high when caught up in their evil ploys. They backstab with the guiltless calm of an assassin taking out a target, spread malicious rumors with the enthusiasm of a potent bull turned loose in a pasture of young heifers, and will sabotage a colleague's work with the malevolence of a politician casting the deciding vote that defeats opposition party members' legislation just to see them lose.

Colleague Slayers are an enigma in a time when terms like *contributive, cooperative,* and *congenial* are bandied about as advantageous attributes. They are destructive, obstinate, and contemptuous.

But Colleague Slayers can be dependable and hardworking when it comes to their own jobs. Amicable and polite when they have to be, they are also protective of close associates.

As managers, Colleague Slayers do not tolerate an interloper's attempt to intrude in their "business" but will casually invade another manager's space without invitation. They also demand obedience and loyalty from their subordinates, and in return will protect them with the ferocious instinct of a lion protecting his pride. And when it comes to meeting their obligations, Colleague Slayers are generally effective managers with an ability to get the best out of the people they work with.

As peers, Colleague Slayers are usually cheerful and cooperative with coworkers who haven't offended them, pose no threat to them, or are willing to help them promote their self-interests. However, they are disdainful toward peers who don't fall under at least one of these categories. In this regard, Colleague Slayers are cavalier. They do not respect their colleagues' privacy or right to carry out their assignments free from petty interference. They also feel that they have to be first among their peers. They do not share the limelight of success unless the greatest light is shining on them. Because of this, they are generally untrustworthy and sneaky combatants in a one-sided game of survival of the strongest.

As subordinates, Colleague Slayers feign loyalty to the boss and outwardly appear to support their coworkers. However, this sly illusion is nothing more than a thin veil projected to mask their dastardly deeds. When opportunities to subvert a colleague present themselves, Colleague Slayers respect neither person nor position; all of their coworkers are fair game. Nevertheless, they are normally competent at their jobs and often possess highly desirable skills and abilities.

The problem in getting along with Colleague Slayers isn't just that they are malicious but also that they know no other way to cope with their own disappointments or to compete for recognition and reward. For this reason, working with Colleague Slayers can be like having a Siberian tiger share your bed; the fear of being eaten makes it hard for you to close your eyes.

If you work for a Colleague Slayer:

- *Do your best.* Colleague Slayer managers expect perfection from their associates despite the fact that perfection is rarely possible or necessary. Regardless, rather than becoming obsessed with attaining perfection, concentrate at doing your best at your assignments. More often than not, your best efforts will produce good enough results to satisfy a Colleague Slayer manager's expectations.

- *Keep your distance.* Becoming the toady of Colleague Slayers will endear you to them, but only until they have no further use for you. It will also make you an accomplice, turn you into a potential scapegoat, and certainly raise suspicions about your ethics. Therefore, while not being able to ignore the boss, you

should keep a safe distance from your boss's villain-
ous activities.

- *Be discrete.* Colleague Slayer managers can be very
  charming. Don't be fooled. Their intent is to charm
  information out of you that can be used against your
  coworkers. Be careful about what you disclose or
  confide to Colleague Slayer managers. A good rule of
  thumb is never to say anything about anyone that
  you wouldn't say to their face or in a crowded room.

If you have a peer who is a Colleague Slayer:

- *Interact on a need-to-know basis.* Colleague Slayers
  will pump you for more information than they need
  to know about your work, but don't be deceived by
  their sweet talk. You should have serious misgivings
  about confiding more to Colleague Slayers than they
  really need to know. Doing so won't make getting
  along with Colleague Slayers difficult, but it will
  keep your relationship with them on a proper level.

- *Keep your small talk small.* Colleague Slayers like to
  engage in small talk about people and listen to others talk about themselves. Small talk is a useful lubri-
  cant in relationships, but it becomes a source of
  friction if used as an occasion to backbite, start or
  spread rumors, or otherwise sabotage colleagues.

- *Safeguard sensitive information.* Colleague Slayers will violate your space, whether or not you are present in your space at the time. Be cautious about leaving sensitive information in a place where it is readily accessible to them, or to anyone else with whom it shouldn't be shared.

- *Expose them.* If you have personal knowledge of Colleague Slayers' nefarious activities, let them know. And should their activities so warrant, report them to the proper person. Colleague Slayers prefer to be invisible instigators and will back off when exposed.

If you manage a Colleague Slayer:

- *Keep them productively occupied.* Colleague Slayers are normally competent and will meet or exceed job-performance expectations. In fact, the ease with which they complete their assignments provides them "free time" to spread discontent. If it appears that Colleague Slayer subordinates have too much time on their hands, assign them more tasks to perform. This will keep their focus on something productive, require less of your time to police their counterproductive behavior, and prevent you from having to deal with the consequences that arise from their unscrupulous activities.

- *Be decisive.* Take decisive action at the first indication that Colleague Slayer subordinates are involved in inappropriate conduct. Allowing it to go on will only make matters worse. This includes putting an end to backbiting, rumors, and sabotage.

- *Discipline justly.* Although most managers would rather not become involved, one of a manager's most important duties is to referee interpersonal conflicts among subordinates in a fair manner. This is often difficult. Very few conflict resolutions are win-win, and no matter how fair you try to be in resolving interpersonal conflicts, someone always seems to walk away feeling that justice hasn't been served. When dealing with conflicts among your staff members, make certain that all involved take ownership of their part in creating the problem and understand their responsibility to end it. If some sort of discipline is warranted, do your best to discipline appropriately to the offense. Doing so will not only hold Colleague Slayers accountable for their behavior, but it will give them less motive to seek retaliation.

- *Keep your personal thoughts positive.* Colleague Slayers often appear to be gregarious and loyal associates in whom you can trustingly confide. Nonetheless, you should always be cautious when speaking freely to Colleague Slayers, because what you say to them can and will be used against you. However, sharing your *positive* personal thoughts about coworkers or other matters can be a tremendous way to build morale. In addition, positive thoughts can't be used against you or others. Conversely, venting negative feelings in the workplace is counterproductive, if not potentially destructive. If you have negative feelings and need to express them, vent them with a trustworthy confidant outside the workplace.

Getting along with Colleague Slayers involves watching your back, front, and sides, which is an unfortunate but necessary measure to prevent them from unduly interfering with your work or destroying your reputation. It also entails helping them understand that bringing others down will lead to their own downfall. And once they realize they can't escape the consequences of their actions, Colleague Slayers tend to improve their workplace behavior.

CHAPTER TWELVE

PRODUCTIVITY REBELS

"The Secretly Defiant"

Cynical and sullen, Productivity Rebels are intentionally ineffective. They seem to have a deep-seated—but essentially arbitrary—sense of anger toward authority figures. They are so stubbornly resistant to being told what to do that they would rather stay in a burning building than take orders from the firefighters trying to rescue them

Productivity Rebels passively express their combative nature by covert obstructionism, pigheadedness, and purposefully wasting time. Having a low level of self-confidence, they are convinced that they are always misunderstood and unappreciated. Productivity Rebels' sulky, gloomy attitudes can make Eeyore in *Winnie the*

Pooh look like a lighthearted optimist. They also believe that fate's fortune doesn't shine on them enough, making them resentful of others whom they perceive to be successful.

Productivity Rebels march to the beat of an unconsciously negative attitude toward life, which makes getting along with them stressful at best and punitive at worst. They are habitually unassertive but employ manipulation and unresponsiveness to routine responsibilities as means of indirectly controlling others. If they are unable to beguile others into doing what they want, Productivity Rebels will refuse to perform, leaving others to pick up their slack. Productivity Rebels are argumentative for no apparent reason and are quick to criticize other people, whether or not the criticism is warranted. But when they feel misunderstood or mistreated themselves, Productivity Rebels resort to pouting bouts of self-pity as a way to gain others' sympathy.

In a world where a work ethic and cooperation are seen as desirable qualities, Productivity Rebels protest even trivial matters ad nauseam and procrastinate until it is too late for their efforts to matter. Yet despite incompetence raised to an art form, Productivity Rebels survive because they are so skillful in gaining others' sympathy, and they escape accountability by masking their intentional impediments to progress in a cloak of contrition.

Productivity Rebels, however, are not necessarily lazy or dissatisfied with their jobs, and they are quite capable of performing all of their tasks. When they take the responsibility to put their self-detrimental behaviors aside, Productivity Rebels have what it takes to make proactive, efficient, and meaningful contributions in the workplace. They simply choose not to do so.

As managers, Productivity Rebels are covertly hostile toward superiors they can neither beguile nor indirectly control. They attempt to develop overly dependent and protective relationships with their subordinates. They spend too much time sharing their pessimistic outlook (what is wrong, unfair, and unappreciated) with their associates, which sows the seeds of despair, saps emotional stamina, and impedes productivity. They are persistently trapped in their web of defiance, which makes these poor decision makers ambivalent and unreliable.

As peers, Productivity Rebels are ostensibly cooperative, but they qualify their cooperation with dawdling, insensibleness, and withholding of important information. They do not openly compete for power or to influence team decisions, but they will undermine team efforts by deliberate ineffectiveness. They also harbor envy for peers they see as receiving more favorable treatment from management, which puts them at odds with most everyone.

As subordinates, Productivity Rebels are very frustrating to manage. They appear to be dedicated to their work; to have a dutiful, can-do attitude; and to possess sufficient skills to accomplish their tasks. But they rarely deliver on their commitments or perform up to their abilities. They also have high ego-maintenance needs: no accomplishment is too trite to go unnoticed, and any slight of appreciation is taken as a blow to their self-worth. They also become agitated when held accountable for missing deadlines or for giving a halfhearted effort in performing their assignments.

The problem in getting along with Productivity Rebels is that they can perform and cooperate; they just don't want to. Most of them have nurtured a festering, irrational anger at authority figures until their anger is as comfortable to them as an old leather jacket. But like Achilles sulking in his tent, Productivity Rebels will perform as soon as they become convinced that doing their job is much more satisfying than wallowing in a mixture of self-pity and silent rage.

If you work for a Productivity Rebel:

- *Be proactive.* Productivity Rebel managers aren't really sure what their boss expects of them, which makes it rather difficult for them to be clear about what they expect from you. And when you don't know what is expected of you, you end up spinning your wheels too much of the time. When you have questions about an assignment, don't expect a Productivity Rebel manager to come up with the answers. Go to their boss and ask for clarification. You don't have to be sneaky about it; just inform your manager that you are going to discuss the assignment with their boss to ensure that you are headed in the right direction. The risk of irritating your manager is far less worrisome than failing to meet the expectations for your work. It will also give you some face time with your boss's boss, which will help him or her become more aware of your commitment to your work and your potential for future opportunities.

- *Remain independent.* You really won't go anywhere by becoming a Productivity Rebel manager's flunky or enabler. Don't "hang out" with a Productivity Rebel manager. Pessimism becomes infectious through frequent exposure to it. Keep your interactions polite but work-related. Do your job, but do not pick up Productivity Rebel managers' slack or assume any of their responsibilities. Besides, doing other people's work doesn't encourage them to become responsible. And if you need a mentor, turn to someone other than a Productivity Rebel manager for advice and counsel. Productivity Rebels are short on good judgment and cannot be relied on to provide you with sensible guidance.

* *Be optimistic.* Optimism prevents you from adopting the dreary attitudes that keep Productivity Rebel managers from ever being successful or happy. Optimism is the stimulant of well-adjusted people. It provides hope in times of despair and a positive attitude for situations calling for clear thinking, and it brightens an otherwise gloomy day. Optimism also causes you to see others for the good they do, which makes getting along with them much easier. Moreover, it will change how a Productivity Rebel manager interacts with you. It's difficult for anyone to be purposefully negative in the company of people who have a positive spirit about them.

If you have a peer who is a Productivity Rebel:

* *Practice proactive damage control.* Productivity Rebels are quick to make commitments on which they plan to default. Such duplicity means that you must make frequent checks to ensure that Productivity Rebels are actually engaged in activities that will result in them meeting their commitments to team projects. If you see that they are intentionally impeding progress on team projects, tell them what tasks you are waiting for them to complete, and make certain

they understand that you have no intention of doing their work. If they continue to dawdle, send them a written memo reminding them of your earlier conversation and the deadlines for their assigned tasks. If this reminder doesn't get them moving in the right direction, let your boss know that there may be a delay in the project because your Productivity Rebel peer is not making proper progress toward the goal. At this point, addressing the problem more forcefully becomes your manager's responsibility.

- *Don't rub your success in their face.* Productivity Rebels are resentful of others who receive more recognition and rewards than they do. Their resentment in this regard is normally expressed by way of a tactless comment or a morose mannerism, neither of which are sufficient enough to cause you to tremble with fear or to keep your success a secret. What's more important is that you remember that your success makes very few of your peers happy for you, and it makes some of them envious of you. But despite your success, you still have to get along with your peers. For this reason, be thankful for peers who share in your happiness, but don't rub your success in the face of peers who are struggling with their assignments or ones whose accomplishments have gone unnoticed.

- *Be generous with appreciation.* Productivity Rebels have a fundamental need to be appreciated. When they feel unappreciated, they sulk. And when they sulk, they think up ways to obstruct your progress. Providing your Productivity Rebel peers with words, and perhaps small tokens, of appreciation for routine efforts on your behalf doesn't take much effort or time, but it will go a long way in feeding their need to be appreciated, which will make them less of an obstruction to you.

If you manage a Productivity Rebel:

- *Teach them to be responsible, not self-defeating.* Productivity Rebels do not know how to deal with their defiant attitude properly. As a result, much of their time and effort is spent engaged in self-defeating activities. Intentional ineffectiveness is the cardinal indication that a subordinate is a Productivity Rebel. The most effective way to deal with Productivity Rebels is to make them aware that you know they are performing below their ability and inform them of the consequences for inadequate performance. Productivity Rebels will deny being guilty of any such transgression, which is only to be expected. Don't argue that point, but do suggest ways for them to think and act more responsibly. Most people believe they have more talent than they actually do, which gives them the self-confidence to take on challenges beyond their abilities and develop new talents in the process. Productivity Rebels consistently perform below their talent level because they suffer from a lack of self-confidence. Teaching them to use their talent responsibly boosts their self-confidence. And when they become more self-confident, Productivity Rebels begin to think and act more positively.

- *Put it in writing.* Productivity Rebels are forgetful because they are preoccupied by cynicism. And forgetting what they were supposed to do becomes an excuse for them not to have done what was agreed on. Putting your instructions to them in writing not only serves as a reminder but also helps clarify your expectations, as Productivity Rebels don't ask questions when they are uncertain of what is expected of them.

- *Supervise them closely.* Productivity Rebels have an aversion to being closely supervised because it prevents them from being able to mask their inefficiency. But close supervision is exactly what Productivity Rebels require if you want them to perform up to their ability. Of course, they will predictably see this as unfair treatment. However, effective supervision means that you supervise every individual's performance appropriately. Productivity Rebels simply require close supervision in order to be effective in their jobs. And when they demonstrate that they are responsible and trustworthy, you can begin to supervise Productivity Rebels less closely.

- *Don't tolerate sulking behavior.* Normal mood swings are to be accepted as an inevitable part of life, as are occasional arguments and quarrels when passion escalates beyond reason. On the other hand, sulking behavior is not something that you should tolerate from Productivity Rebels or any other subordinate. Ask them about the nature of the problem. Be supportive, and do what you can to address their problem appropriately. However, do not address their demands in a way that sanctions sulking behavior as an acceptable response to workplace problems.

Getting along with Productivity Rebels involves helping them realize that covert defiance closes the door of opportunity to them. It also requires that you not allow their negativism to turn you into someone you would rather not be. And the sooner Productivity Rebels are confronted with the consequences of their maladaptive behavior and shoddy job performance, the quicker they will begin adopting sensible behavior and improving the quality of their work.

CHAPTER THIRTEEN

TEMPERAMENTAL TYRANTS

"The Happiness-Impaired"

Unstable and disgruntled, Temperamental Tyrants always appear to be mad at the world in general. If not furious over one thing, they are looking for something to get peeved about. They are so teeming with inner rage that they make Vlad the Impaler seem like Santa Claus.

Temperamental Tyrants are so cantankerous and volatile that they can burst into a tirade at the least provocation. They are never truly happy, even in the most fortunate circumstances, which makes it extremely difficult for them to form healthy interpersonal relationships. They are easily offended but are unforgiving themselves. Temperamental Tyrants are also vindictive, and they place no statute of limitations on exacting their own brand of justice. It's not unusual for Temperamental Tyrants to execute acts of retaliation against their offenders at the first opportunity, even if the opportune time occurs so long after the crime that they can't recall the specifics of the offense.

Temperamental Tyrants are extraordinarily high-strung and have the impulse control of a junkyard dog. They will attack anyone who intrudes on their space, which makes them socially awkward and uncomfortable in team settings. And, like a junkyard dog, Temperamental Tyrants need a skilled handler if they are to keep from biting the hand that feeds them. Moreover, when it comes to acting on their hostility, Temperamental Tyrants' actions aren't always arbitrated by common sense. As such, they often injure the innocent in an attempt to harm their offenders. In this regard, Temperamental Tyrants are combative to a fault, preferring a Pyrrhic victory to a mutual truce that would commit them to more adaptive behavior in the ordinary give-and-take of work life.

Temperamental Tyrants are out of place in a world where patience, understanding, and impulse control are considered important interpersonal qualities. They are restless, hard-hearted, and reckless.

That said, Temperamental Tyrants are also usually technically competent and conscientious in meeting their job responsibilities. They can also be excellent mentors who will make time to help others develop their skills or solve problems. And when composed, Temperamental Tyrants can be civilized and proper people.

As managers, Temperamental Tyrants are preoccupied with authority (exercising theirs and yielding to that of powerful superiors) and meeting goals; they are easily irritated by anyone or anything that interrupts or distracts their preoccupation. They give directions more often than they sell ideas, and frequently their minds are made up before they ask others for their opinions. Temperamental Tyrants are also reluctant to manage self-confident, well-connected subordinates, which is reflected in their hiring and staffing decisions.

As peers, Temperamental Tyrants are uncomfortable in team settings because they know that most people would rather avoid them than work with them. They view their peers as competitors for their manager's affection and approval. Amid ordinary, honest, and open debate with their peers, Temperamental Tyrants become aggressive rather than convincing because their warlike predisposition obscures their ability to follow the logic of the argument. And when they don't prevail in an argument, Temperamental Tyrants withdraw and become uncooperative.

As subordinates, Temperamental Tyrants are doggedly obedient to influential members of management, which may or may not include their own manager. It all depends on what being obedient to their manager offers them. The more their manager can potentially provide them, the more loyal Temperamental Tyrants become. They are a bit stubborn in their ways, but Temperamental Tyrants are often conscientious workers who can be depended on to fulfill their assignments reasonably well. Nonetheless, Temperamental Tyrants do not have sufficient emotional control to be trusted to handle high-stress situations.

The problem in getting along with Temperamental Tyrants isn't that they vent their spleen some of the time but that you never know when or why they will explode. In fact, working with Temperamental Tyrants is like petting a rattlesnake: you're sure to be bitten; it's just a matter of when.

If you work for a Temperamental Tyrant:

- *Show some courage.* Although it can be worrisome to approach Temperamental Tyrant managers on routine matters and unnerving to confront them with serious issues, they aren't as fearsome as they seem. Temperamental Tyrant managers do yell a lot, and few people like to be yelled at in the normal course of their workday. That notwithstanding, don't allow the possibility of being yelled at to stop you from doing the right thing—your job. If you muster up the courage to discuss any work-related issue with Temperamental Tyrant managers, remain levelheaded should they lose composure, keep your discussion issue-oriented, and they will usually calm down quickly and deal with you and your issue responsibly. Moreover, once Temperamental Tyrant managers understand that you are not afraid of them, they will become more civil with you.

- *Refuse to be abused.* Temperamental Tyrants are known to take out their frustrations on others as a way of coping with their general state of unhappiness. Not only is this an abuse of management authority, it is a violation of people's basic right to civil treatment in the workplace. Any manager can be grumpy on a bad day, which is no cause for alarm. However, you don't have to suffer Temperamental Tyrant managers' maladaptive moodiness every day. If they are taking out too many of their frustrations on you, tell them to stop. Standing up for your dignity often puts an end to such abuse because even Temperamental Tyrant managers are aware that a reputation for abusing subordinates does not make friends in high places and will alienate them from virtually everyone at work.

- *Try to sense their mood.* Although it can change without warning, trying to sense Temperamental Tyrants' mood before a meeting is always advisable. Getting a sense of their mood is not all that difficult. Ask their assistant or your coworkers. Chances are that one of them will be able to give you a fairly accurate reading. Armed with this information, you will be better able to judge how Temperamental Tyrant managers will react to whatever your business is with them. If you can't get a sense of their mood in advance, err on the side of caution and begin with lighter issues before going into heavier matters. And if you sense that they are losing control, cut your agenda short, wrap up quickly, and give them time to cool off; then, later pick up where you left off. Remember: even the best news won't go over well when your manager is in a bad mood, and the worst news goes over better when your manager is in a good mood.

- *Take the opportunity to learn something new.* Temperamental Tyrant managers are successful not because of their people skills but because of their competence. Asking a Temperamental Tyrant manager to explain something you don't totally understand but would like to know more about is a good way to build a positive work relationship with them. It flatters them to be asked to share their know-how. More often than not, if they don't have time to teach you right away, they will make time at their earliest convenience. Temperament Tyrants are conscientious in carrying out their responsibilities, and this trait spawns a willingness to help their subordinates become better at their jobs. Moreover, besides helping you perform better in the present, learning something new prepares you for future career opportunities.

If you have a peer who is a Temperamental Tyrant:

- *Avoid needless conflict.* Temperamental Tyrants do not mitigate their emotions with reason, which causes them to overreact to petty opposition as well as to significant differences of opinion. They are inclined to retaliate against those who offend them, especially in public settings. None of this should bother you if you have an honest difference of opinion, a dispute that should be aired, or an otherwise prudent reason to confront Temperamental Tyrant peers. On the other hand, avoiding needless conflicts with Temperamental Tyrant peers is also prudent, as they will create more problems for you to deal with than you will want to spend your time and energy addressing.

- *Recognize normal mood swings.* All people have good and bad days that affect their disposition accordingly. This is not maladaptive conduct but normal behavior. This truth also applies to Temperamental Tyrants, whose normal mood swings should be recognized and tolerated just like everyone else's. Although Temperamental Tyrants' moods are difficult to disregard at times, if you become too sensitive to their mood swings it places excessive emphasis on their disposition and not enough emphasis on your work-related activities with them. It also gives Temperamental Tyrants' moods too much influence over your own productivity. Recognize normal mood swings for what they are, and never make more out of them than you should.

- *Let them save face.* Temperament Tyrants do have a sense of shame, which often causes them to withdraw after a particularly embarrassing outburst, and it's difficult to interact with peers when they feel sheepish about being in your presence. When one of these situations arises, just act as if your Temperamental Tyrant peers did nothing to be embarrassed about and conduct your business with them as usual. They will still realize that you know differently but will appreciate your acting as if you didn't. Letting Temperamental Tyrants save face is a persuasive method for bringing them out of a spell of self-imposed isolation and for getting your activities with them back on track.

- *Sometimes it's best to turn the other cheek.* Temperamental Tyrants are uncomfortable in team settings and become agitated and argumentative as a result of their personal discomfort more often than they do over work-related differences. When Temperamental Tyrants blow up at you over something seemingly trivial and not worth fighting about, sometimes it's best not to respond but just to sit or stand there and let them rant and rave. Verbally abusing someone who refuses to get caught up in the fray is a humiliating experience that few people will persist at. Moreover, turning the other cheek is often an effective method for helping Temperamental Tyrants become aware of their inappropriate behavior, which is a good thing for them and you.

If you manage a Temperamental Tyrant:

- *Discipline maladaptive behavior.* More often than not, Temperamental Tyrants persist in self-destructive and disruptive behavior because no one holds them accountable for their maladaptive conduct. If you discipline Temperamental Tyrants the first time they get out of control, you will be sending them a strong message about your unwillingness to let such behavior go unnoticed or unpenalized. And because word gets around, it will broadcast a warning to the rest of your subordinates that you will not condone inappropriate behavior in general.

- *Help them become self-aware.* Temperamental Tyrants are often unaware of the consequences of their tirades, which can inflict emotional harm on others and place limits on their own success. A good opportunity to teach Temperamental Tyrants the value of managing their anger occurs just after the dust has settled from one of their emotional explosions. Explain how you and others interpreted their outburst. Tell them how their outburst is affecting their relationship with you and others. And last but not least, confront them with the consequences of continued outbursts. Indeed, real behavior change cannot begin until there is an awareness of the behavior that needs changing.

- *Use their skills wisely.* Temperamental Tyrants often possess expertise that will benefit them and you when used appropriately. Temperamental Tyrants want to do something meaningful, and when they feel underutilized they become even more irritable than they normally are. Moreover, when Temperamental

Tyrants are doing something that makes them feel as if their skills are being put to proper use, the curtain that hides their ability to be happy begins to fall.

- *Be of good cheer.* Nothing speaks louder or more clearly to people than their manager's behavior. If you are cheerful most of the time, it's likely that your subordinates will imitate your example. The same is true if you are sullen most of the time. And as Temperamental Tyrants are not exempt from this fact of life, the more cheerful you are in dealing with them, the more you can expect them to act just like you.

Getting along with Temperamental Tyrants requires you to learn how to show grace in the face of capricious fire, to keep calm when you might be justified in being angry, and to help them become more self-aware. It also involves allowing them no escape or excuse for their tirades or acts of retaliation. Temperamental Tyrants really need to understand that there is no acceptable alternative to civilized behavior in the workplace. And when you give Temperamental Tyrants no way out of being held accountable for their conduct, it's amazing how quickly they can learn to control their habitual tendencies.

CHAPTER FOURTEEN

TOUCHY-FEELIES

"The Social Workers"

Hypersensitive and meddlesome, Touchy-Feelies are altruistic, fanatical members of the self-esteem police who issue excuses for helpless coworkers. They are so concerned about everyone "feeling good" that in a war they would charge the enemy lines armed with self-help books and try to talk about the opposing soldiers' feelings.

Touchy-Feelies have fragile egos and are fussy and terribly insecure. They are often affectionate for the wrong reasons, and place too much emphasis on their need for social acceptance and recognition. They are easily frustrated and tend to resist authority. Touchy-Feelies hold fast to the notion that everyone must like everyone else in order to work well together. They ruminate too much over small, petty details, which causes them to worry about things that shouldn't be worried about and takes their attention away from more serious matters that they should be concerned with.

Touchy-Feelies are stubborn do-gooders who feel obligated to come to the aid of coworkers who can't deal with workplace setbacks, the fact that they can't always have their way, or the negative consequences of failing to perform. But by intervening in situations where they feel someone isn't being treated fairly, Touchy-Feelies actually weave more interpersonal tension than they untangle. And it matters not to Touchy-Feelies if the situation is one in which they have no legitimate voice or no knowledge of the facts, or if appropriate measures are already being taken to correct a problem.

Touchy-Feelies are out of place in a world where self-reliance, personal responsibility, and emotional toughness are highly valued traits. They attempt to make their coworkers beholden to them by involving themselves in other people's business and creating an environment of emotional dependency.

Touchy-Feelies also have a tendency to be perfectionists. They are generally adequate performers when working in jobs that give them a high degree of freedom from close supervision and scrutinized accountability.

As managers, Touchy-Feelies emphasize impressions and appearances rather than people and productivity. Self-sacrificing, they will do the work of poor-performing but otherwise capable associates to prevent them from experiencing the contrary consequences of personal negligence. They have a tendency to develop harmonious relationships among their associates and are so overly protective of them that they will overlook behavior that warrants disciplinary action.

As peers, Touchy-Feelies are excessive caretakers who are overbearing in their efforts to make their coworkers feel happy. Illusory happiness always masks real problems, and dealing with real problems is never fun for Touchy-Feelies. They also tend to meddle in their coworkers' personal lives. Touchy-Feelies will try to rescue coworkers from unpleasant situations and will always provide them with an out so that they don't have to take any responsibility for being part of their own problems.

As subordinates, Touchy-Feelies exhibit excessive devotion to their boss but become anxiety-ridden when they feel the least bit slighted or unappreciated. When feeling rejected, Touchy-Feelies become sullen and withdrawn, fail to complete tasks on time, and are easily overwhelmed by a normal workload. And when overwhelmed, they are reluctant to ask for help because they see their role in life as helping others.

The problem in getting along with Touchy-Feelies isn't that they are do-gooders but that they inappropriately enmesh themselves in matters beyond the scope of their responsibilities. Frankly, Touchy-Feelies can be as agitating as fans at a sporting event who block your view with signs bearing biblical references. Their intentions are good, but they don't know when to leave well enough alone.

If you work for a Touchy-Feely:

- *Help them stay focused.* Touchy-Feely managers would rather talk about imaginary people problems than concentrate their efforts on guiding and directing the real work under their supervision. Although people problems can be distracting and disruptive, Touchy-Feely managers make more of them than necessary. To avoid being bogged down by needless diversions, keep your discussions with Touchy-Feely managers focused on getting your job done. This will not only help you stay on track but will help your Touchy-Feely manager concentrate more on what is really important.

- *Be generous with appreciation.* Oddly enough, Touchy-Feely managers crave frequent tokens of appreciation from all of their coworkers. Showing appreciation for their support and assistance will go a long way in helping you maintain a healthy relationship with a Touchy-Feely manager. If you don't show appreciation, Touchy-Feely managers will resent you.

- *Feed their need to control.* You don't have to become a submissive wimp to get along with Touchy-Feely managers, but you do need to make them feel as if they are totally in charge. Keep them constantly informed of your activities and get their okay before starting new projects. Despite their rigidity, Touchy-Feelies can be rather flexible if you make them believe that they are in charge.

- *Mind your manners.* Although Touchy-Feely managers are prone to overlooking inappropriate behavior (which actually enables such behavior to recur), you can count on other members of management not being so forgiving. By keeping your workplace behavior appropriate, you will avoid having to worry about other members of management stepping in when a Touchy-Feely manager is reluctant to handle the situation.

If you have a peer who is a Touchy-Feely:

- *Keep your private life private.* Because you spend so much of your time at work, it's always comforting to have a coworker who will listen to your personal problems. That notwithstanding, discussing your private life at work can backfire. It is especially risky with Touchy-Feelies, as they tend to develop fatal attractions. You must remember that ordinary life is fraught with difficulties, and there are no logical reasons for turning your personal difficulties into a nightmare by sharing them with a Touchy-Feely.

- *Keep them uninvited to your business.* Touchy-Feelies have a tendency to involve themselves in their coworkers work-related affairs. You don't have to be rude, but a polite "Thank you, but I am perfectly capable of dealing with this situation" is a good way to put an end to their meddling. If they don't take the hint, use a more direct approach.

- *Encourage them to be responsible.* Touchy-Feelies are often so immersed in office politics that they neglect their own assignments. If you compensate for their negligence, Touchy-Feelies will become even more negligent. Touchy-Feelies require a lot of encouragement to stay on task. However, if you can see that a Touchy-Feely peer is going to miss a deadline that relates to your work, inform your manager about the current situation and possible delays so that your manager can take corrective action.

If you manage a Touchy-Feely:

- *Establish expectations and deadlines.* Touchy-Feelies are not self-directing, which means that they require very clear expectations and deadlines in order to get on track and stay there until the task is completed. Keep them on a short leash. If tethered to a long rope, Touchy-Feelies will wander away from their work and can get tangled in matters unrelated to their real responsibilities.

- *Watch your back.* Touchy-Feelies do not have a combative countenance, which is why they can catch you off guard. Nevertheless, if they feel threatened by having to account for their own inadequate performance, they will go to your boss behind your back in a heartbeat and blame you for all their work-related problems. In the absolute, there is little you can do to prevent this kind of behavior; you just have to deal with it when it happens. Fortunately, most senior managers are familiar with these tactics and don't condone blame-avoidance behavior.

- *Praise results.* Touchy-Feelies often have low self-esteem, which gives them a sense of powerlessness. If you properly praise their accomplishments, it can help them overcome these emotional shortcomings. In praising results, remember that self-esteem doesn't grow on excuses, and making excuses for inadequate performance simply validates personal powerlessness. Conversely, adequate performance builds self-esteem and provides a sense of personal power. Keep in mind that the results don't need to be perfect to be praise-worthy, just simply good enough.

- *Don't excuse them from reality.* Touchy-Feelies don't deal well with the unpleasant situations that attend normal work life. Rather than taking concrete steps to steer bad situations toward a more positive direction, Touchy-Feelies adopt counterproductive coping mechanisms that spawn distorted fears, needless anxiety, and irrational thought processes. Excusing them from having to deal with the negative doesn't make them stronger or make the problem go away; instead it gives rise to excuse making and more negligence. To develop their self-confidence in dealing with such a predicament, talk Touchy-Feelies through it in a reassuring manner. Tell them that you're not looking for someone to blame but want to help them become more self-reliant in dealing with adversity. In addition, let them know that you expect them to deal with ordinary problems in a positive way.

Getting along with Touchy-Feelies is a matter of helping them reshape their distorted image as caretakers of happiness and weaning them from their constant need for attention. Once it is understood that taking care of their own work is job one, Touchy-Feelies will realize that they earn appreciation when they complete their work.

CHAPTER FIFTEEN

FREQUENT FLIERS
"The Entitlement Chasers"

Shortsighted and self-justifying, Frequent Fliers have an addiction for using their organization's resources as if they were their own. They are so intellectually dishonest that they wouldn't hesitate to expense a holiday party, complete with nice gifts, for their friends and neighbors.

Frequent Fliers are users with a self-serving idea of right and wrong. They have situational ethics and believe that the rules they break or the policies they violate don't apply to them. They are also accomplished rationalizers. Thus, they have a clear conscience when indulging in unauthorized use of their expense accounts, making personal use of their organization's tools and equipment, helping themselves to office supplies, or performing any other illicit activity that feeds their habit of fiscal corruption.

Frequent Fliers are individualistic, shallow, and greedy. They have a relentless pattern of serving their own interests first and foremost—an interpersonal style that routinely infringes on the rights and violates the trust of others. They become flushed and flustered in situations where they can't abuse their access to organizational resources for personal gain. And they get defensive when confronted with their transgressions, after which others often grant them immunity, as Frequent Fliers are masters of denial.

Frequent Fliers are a paradox in a world where intellectual integrity, good judgment, humility, and selflessness are touted as desirable personal values because they are indeed deceitful, shortsighted, conceited, and self-centered.

On the other hand, Frequent Fliers are often otherwise dutiful to their jobs and loyal to their organization. They tend to know how to maneuver their way through bureaucratic red tape, which can be a very desirable skill. They also have an amazing ability to read people well enough to anticipate how others will react in most situations.

As managers, Frequent Fliers are responsible and reliable in carrying out their basic management tasks. They are usually willing to delegate both details and authority to capable subordinates on whom they feel they can depend. However, they show poor judgment when it comes to exercising their discretionary authority over funds, associates' time, and other resources that can be put to their personal use.

As peers, Frequent Fliers are generally dependable and likable teammates. They tend to be outgoing, pleasant, and quite easy to work with. However, they are charming moochers more devoted to what they can get you to do for them than they are committed to doing something for you. And when they do a small favor for you, they always expect a larger favor from you in return.

As subordinates, Frequent Fliers don't go out of their way to create problems, but they exhibit difficulty in following directions or playing by the rules. They can be solid performers if carefully supervised, but they are easily distracted by opportunities to enrich themselves unjustly. And regardless of their regular pay and perks, they feel deprived of their full due and will resort to unacceptable means to make up the perceived difference.

The problem in getting along with Frequent Fliers isn't just their fixation with padding their pockets but also that in padding their pockets they divert people's time and the organization's resources away from their intended use. Indeed, working with Frequent Fliers can be as aggravating as paying a neighborhood teen to mow your lawn only to have the kid take your mower home after the job is done. However, there are practical ways to deal with Frequent Fliers without having to compromise your principles or condone their misconduct.

If you work for a Frequent Flier:

- *Sidestep doing personal favors.* Frequent Flier managers often ask close associates to run personal errands or do personal favors for them. For the most part, they expect these requests to be met during normal work hours and at the organization's expense. That such requests fall outside your legitimate duties makes them an abuse of Frequent Flier managers' authority. Although it is easy to get caught up in doing favors for managers because they become more willing to make special allowances for you in return, there is no job security or future in becoming a designated favor performer. If you want to be valued enough to remain on the payroll during hard times or to be considered for a promotion, it is far better to do your job well than to do special favors or run errands for your manager. And, as Frequent Flier managers are aware that asking an associate to perform personal favors is inappropriate, they usually won't become upset when you politely refuse to accommodate such requests.

- *Take the ball and run.* As Frequent Flier managers are prone to delegating both details and authority, working for one presents you with a terrific opportunity to put your talents on display. Take advantage of such situations; you won't have enough of them in your career to bypass the ones that come your way. Just keep your Frequent Flier managers informed about your plans and progress so that they won't be embarrassed if asked about your activities. If you run into a bureaucratic roadblock along the way, consult your Frequent Flier managers for advice on how to get around it without alienating people you are going to have to work with the next day. Of course, Frequent Flier managers will lay claim to a lot of the recognition and rewards that will accompany your successful accomplishment of your goals. But don't worry too much about this fact of work life. Others will know who got the job done, and getting the job done will always yield opportunities for you to advance your career.

- *Wear your ethics.* Frequent Flier managers are adept at talking others into doing things they know they shouldn't do. If you are not mindful, they can talk you into misusing your budget or other resources to serve their self-interests. However, if Frequent Flier managers understand that you won't disrespect the trust that others have placed in you, they will be less likely to ask you to make illegitimate use of your resources on their behalf. Even so, there are situations when what you are being asked to do falls into a gray area, which makes knowing what to do unclear at the time. Such situations present you with a difficult choice—one that can affect your relationship with your manager or affect your career. Either way, always be willing to live with your choice in these matters, because no decision involving money and other resources can be kept secret for long. Moreover, if you choose poorly, Frequent Flier managers are not going to accept responsibility for having convinced you to step out on a limb for their selfish benefit when your course of action becomes known.

If you have a peer who is a Frequent Flier:

- *Be cautious about reporting misuse of resources.* Frequent Fliers are unhampered users of organizational resources and tend to believe that throwing money at a problem will make it go away. Wasteful spending is a sign of poor judgment, not unethical conduct. At the same time, poor judgment mixed with self-serving ideas of right and wrong can lead to corrupt behavior. Although the observable difference between poor judgment and unethical conduct seems an easy enough distinction, it is not. Perceptions can be very misleading and can cause you to misjudge what you believe to be true. Therefore, if you believe that Frequent Flier peers are involved in illicit use of organizational resources, make certain that you can support your belief with fact. Making a false report about peers' ethical conduct will harm your reputation and standing. But, oddly enough, a truthful report may also damage your relationships in the workplace. The choice to report or overlook misuse of organizational resources is not as easy in real life as it is in a training exercise. Regardless, if you decide to report what appears to be Frequent Flier peers' fiscal misconduct, be discreet about it. And remember: once you've made your report, the matter becomes someone else's responsibility to deal with.

- *Refuse to be an accomplice.* Frequent Flier peers are quite capable of talking you into doing for them what you wouldn't do for other coworkers. Such things can involve the unauthorized use of funds, equipment, supplies, services, or your associates' time. And to be certain about it, compromising your integrity can be easier than many people believe it to be. Just remember that once you cross integrity's line for Frequent Flier peers, you become their accomplice. Furthermore, as accomplices rarely go unpunished when the real perpetrator goes down, it is always prudent to decide beforehand just how far you are willing to bend the rules to get along with peers. Also bear in mind that Frequent Fliers are sensitive to others' impressions of them. So when you feel that

Frequent Flier peers have infringed on your rights or violated your trust, discuss it with them. Doing so may not be a cure for such behavior in the long term, but it will usually fix the immediate problem, and sometimes that is the best you can expect.

- *Refrain from becoming petty.* Frequent Fliers regularly talk their managers into making special allowances of the financial kind for them. Seeing self-centered peers enjoy exceptional perks is upsetting at best and enraging at worst. Nevertheless, work life never has been and will never be absolutely fair. And making the most of unfair situations always requires more from the person who gets the short end of the stick. Becoming petty over trivial allowances that your manager makes for peers, but not for you, diminishes your character. So if you decide to make an issue out of being left out of special allowances of the financial kind, make certain that what you are protesting is substantial enough to confront your manager over. Otherwise, not complaining is a better option in these situations.

If you manage a Frequent Flier:

- *Set a proper example.* Personal behavior is the clearest expression of a manager's character. If you expect your associates to use organizational resources properly, you can underline this expectation by your own example. If you use your resources appropriately, most of your associates will do the same. If you misuse resources for personal gain, it is very likely that the more impressionable of your associates will follow your lead. However, as Frequent Fliers have their own idea of right and wrong, sometimes it is best to embellish your personal example with a very blunt warning about the consequences of infringing on others' rights or violating one's financial authority or access to organizational property.

- *Teach them to exercise good judgment.* Frequent Fliers have a diminished ability to understand how to use their discretionary authority correctly. Therefore, giving Frequent Fliers a blank check or free access to other organizational resources is a big mistake. Once they do something unethical and get away with it, they will see that their position allows them that kind of freedom; at that point Frequent Fliers often become entangled in their own web of corruption. Teaching Frequent Fliers how to assess, discern, choose, and act in situations where they are entrusted to use organizational resources properly requires a lot of patience, coaching, and some micro-management at first. But as they are usually respon-sible in nonfinancial matters, teaching them fiscal responsibility can be well worth your time and effort.

- *Accept nothing less than their best performance.* Frequent Fliers cut corners when they can, which often results in sloppy work. To get the best performance out of Frequent Fliers, never accept anything less than what they are capable of accomplishing. Confronting Frequent Fliers with their underperformance and insisting that they redo a task until it is acceptable sends a powerful message that you know they can do better and will accept nothing less.

- *Decide where to draw the line.* Managing Frequent Fliers can be a troubling experience. For the most part, they tend to be good workers, and good workers aren't easily replaced. On the other hand, they can do things that put you in a position where you will be the judge and jury that decides their future. Although it is impossible to anticipate all misuses of organizational resources, it's wise to have some idea of how you will react to general types of corruption. And because it's often gut wrenching to be forced to deal with other people's self-inflicted problems, letting your associates know where you draw the line between appropriate and inappropriate conduct will help keep most of them on the side of the line that you don't have to deal with.

Getting along with Frequent Fliers requires that you not become caught up in their web of corruption. It is also a matter of helping them understand the difference between authorized and unauthorized use of organizational resources, and the consequences that come with violating one's authority and other people's trust. And when they know that the rules apply to them, Frequent Fliers tend to comply with the rules everyone else is expected to follow.

AFTERWORD

Being the type of person others don't want to avoid is also important in developing and maintaining mutually beneficial workplace relationships.

During my career, I have had the opportunity to work in some terrific organizations. Nevertheless, I never worked in one where people were free from the challenges of trying to make the most of their relationships with the character types presented in this book.

I have also had the privilege of working with a lot of outstanding people whom I never tried to avoid and who I made every effort not to disappoint. Although these people had plenty of individual differences, they seemed to share some common qualities that made it much easier for others to get along with them. And despite the tendency to believe that outstanding people possess mystical qualities beyond the reach of the majority, the qualities manifested by those I worked with are accessible to all. I also believe that their qualities are worthy of your consideration as you initiate and keep up productive workplace relationships as a manager, as a peer, and as a subordinate.

As a manager:

- *Communicate.* Give your associates your undivided attention when you're talking to them and when you're listening to what they have to say. Be accessible. Never demean. Be willing to discuss brutally frank or extremely sensitive issues. And always keep confidences confidential.

- *Stand by your associates.* Cheer for them when they do well, encourage them when they are struggling, empathize with them when they are suffering, and always be willing to act on their behalf.

- *Forgive honest mistakes.* Forgiving your subordinates' honest mistakes actually enhances their future performance. It also adds fuel to the fire of their enthusiasm, encourages their initiative, and helps build their feelings of self-worth.

- *Show appreciation.* Sincere expression of your appreciation for an honest effort or a job well done will do more to bond productive relationships with your associates than perhaps any other single thing you can do. Never underestimate the value of a simple "Thank you" in welding together relationships that will weather great trials.

As a peer:

- *Be an ally.* Everyone has enough foes to keep them on guard. When your peers consider you their ally, they will let down their guard and become more open and cooperative with you. And make no mistake: just one ally can help you succeed in situations where you could fail on your own.

- *Don't quibble.* Curiously, it is far more common for a relationship to break down as the cumulative result of petty bickering than as a result of heated disagreement over things that really matter. Therefore, arguing with your peers should be reserved for consequential issues. And when all has been said that really needs to be, let go and move on.

- *Be objective.* Being judgmental of your peers only alienates their affection for you. Keep your interactions with them positively focused. Downplay individual differences that are easy to judge but are of no real consequence to your or their success.

- *Compete fairly.* Peers compete in every workplace. People who compete and win fairly rarely earn the resentment of their peers. Although it has been said that "winning is everything," no prize is more valuable than your dignity.

As a subordinate:

- *Do your job.* Nothing will endear you more to your manager or coworkers than simply doing your job and doing it well. Be dependable. Be thorough. And never overlook the unmistakable fact that being good at your job is the quickest way for you to climb any career ladder.

- *Be cheerful.* A cheerful attitude both attracts people to you and gets a lot of your shortcomings overlooked. No one likes a cantankerous contrary, but virtually everyone appreciates those who bear their trials well.

- *Don't be a burden.* Refrain from burdening your manager or coworkers with questions you needn't ask, for guidance and direction you don't need, or by keeping them more informed about your activities than they need or want to be.

- *Abide by rules meant to be obeyed.* There is no famine of advice telling you to have the courage to break the rules. However, the practical reality of breaking rules that are meant to be obeyed is that doing so causes others to have to rein in your behavior, and usually lands you in the penalty box.

And last but not least:

If there is one quality outstanding people share in common it is their general attitude toward life. They are cheerful and not easily discouraged. They deal with problems that can be solved and accept those that are beyond resolution. They look for the best in others and are not overly critical of anyone's shortcomings. They work to make a living but live to enjoy life with significant others. And while they are serious when they have to be, they maintain a sense of humor even when experiencing adversity's trials.

Adopting such an attitude is not sufficient to make you a hero—someone who always wins and never loses. But it will go a long way in helping you become someone whom other people rarely go out of their way to avoid. And when it comes to workplace relationships, that is as good as it gets.

ABOUT THE AUTHOR

Wess Roberts's books have been published in twenty-five languages. He makes his home in Utah, where he writes and speaks on leadership and personal development and manages an executive coaching practice.